Sacraments of War:
The Sword and the Warrior Wash

David L. Bachelor

David L. Bachelor

ACKNOWLEDGMENTS

Bible translations used in this work:

Scripture quotations marked "ESV" are from The Holy Bible, English Standard Version, copyright ©2001 by Crossway Bibles, a publishing ministry of Good News Publishers. Used by permission. All rights reserved.

Scripture quotations marked "BBE" are taken from The Bible in Basic English. This translation is in the public domain.

Scripture quotations marked "CEV" are taken from the Contemporary English Version © 1995 by American Bible Society. Used by permission.

Scripture quotations marked "GNB" are taken from the Good News Bible – Second Edition © 1992 by American Bible Society. Used by permission.

Scripture quotations marked "AT" are the author's (David Bachelor) translation of the verses listed.

Scripture quotations marked "GW" are taken from GOD'S WORD®, © 1995 God's Word to the Nations. Used by permission of Baker Publishing Group.

Scripture quotations marked "MKJV" are taken from the Holy Bible, Modern King James Version
Copyright © 1962 – 1998 By Jay P. Green, Sr. Used by permission of the copyright holder.

In this book any Scripture quotation that is not identified by translation is taken from the MKJV.

Cover created by:

Bob Graves
PortraitEFX - North San Antonio
PO Box 276681
San Antonio, Texas 78227
(210) 591-8646

vi

PART I

1

CURRICULUM VITAE

"God *is* my strength *and* power, and He makes my way perfect. *He* makes my feet like hinds' *feet*, and causing me to stand on my high places. He teaches my hands to war, so that my hands may bend a bow of bronze. (2 Sam 22:33-35)

The Bible reveals that there are many spiritual gifts. My spiritual gift is war. Predictably "war" is missing from the list modern churches use to assess someone's spiritual usefulness. I will admit the spiritual gift of war has a legacy of fratricide that includes the Crusades and the Thirty Years War, but its fruit also contains the freedoms won through the Civil War and World War Two. It is with the awareness of past tragedies that I make this apologia for the warrior as a servant of Jesus Christ. I am not calling the Christian community to embrace crusading again, but merely asking for permission to bring back from secularism a vocation that is found throughout God's word to his people, even to the followers of Jesus Christ. I believe the Church is the only place where those with the gift of war can learn how to serve God both on and off the battlefield. The secular world cannot teach this to our people.

My vocation to war started when I was a child. Whether it was reading chronicles of ancient conflicts or conditioning my body in the gym or spending time on the rifle range, I was like an acolyte preparing for holy orders. My novitiate occurred during my junior year of high school which I spent as an exchange student. The host nation was engaged in a guerilla war. Although I was just a temporary visitor, I was issued a cadet uniform and taught the basics of close order drill. My instructors were war veterans who highlighted their lessons with lashes from their rattan canes. Though merely a cadet, they impressed upon me that waging war was a deadly serious business. After this unexpectedly harsh initiation I knew I had nothing to fear when I returned to the States and joined the U.S. Army.

The Drill Sergeants at Basic Training were all veterans of Vietnam and they taught me infantry skills from the perspective of South East Asia. After Infantry School I was assigned to a mechanized infantry unit. We constantly rehearsed the battle drills necessary to achieve victory against a Soviet invasion of Western Europe. While on active duty I also earned Airborne Wings, the Ranger Tab, and promotions. Unfortunately the U.S. government could not provide me with a war so, after six years in a peacetime army, I left the U.S. military to practice my vocation in the private sector.

I learned that without combat experience it was not as easy to gain access to shadow warfare as I thought it would be. So I abandoned my quest for quasi-military service and began a career in law enforcement at the federal level. Ironically this was the right path to combat and my first war happened in a little place called Los Angeles. Combat started on the afternoon a jury acquitted the police officers responsible for beating Rodney King. By nightfall the city was burning. To help restore order the first President Bush sent federal officers to Southern California and I was among those selected. When our tactical response team arrived in the City of Angels the orange glow of fire colored the entire western sky. A dusk-to-dawn curfew had emptied the usually crowded L.A. freeway system and added to the sense of the supernatural. The combination of fire and empty freeways made me feel like I was driving into a scene from the Apocalypse. Over the next few days I saw mayhem I had expected to see on foreign battlefields, not in my own country.

The supernatural qualities of this deployment to LA opened my awareness to a second calling on my life. I began to volunteer at my church and even spent a summer as a foreign missionary. About a year after the riots I decided it was time to pursue this other call on a full-time basis. So I left federal service to pursue a seminary degree and ordination as a Methodist Minister. The journey took me to Southern Methodist University (SMU) in Dallas and later to England where I was ordained. I served five rural churches in southwestern England as my first pastoral appointment. From

England, God called me to New Mexico. In 2001 my family and I settled into the parsonage of a United Methodist church in the mountains outside Albuquerque. The church had no radio or television reception so when the attacks of September 11th happened I just closed the church and went home to watch the tragedy unfold. Like most Americans I took stock of myself to see what I could offer my country.

When I contacted the Army to see if I could re-join their ranks as a chaplain, they told me that I would be put back in the infantry first and then transferred (at some later date) into the chaplain corps. I jokingly tell people that was how God used the Army to tell me to be a Navy chaplain. In addition to its sailors, the Navy also provides chaplains to the U.S. Marines Corps. In November of 2004 I arrived in Iraq as a chaplain to a Marine attack aviation squadron during the battle for Fallujah. In addition to our main base at Al Asad, I was tasked to support other smaller bases in Anbar Province. What I remember most about this deployment was the makeshift armor all the units were adding to their vehicles. Our convoys looked like a scene from the movie, "The Road Warrior."

I returned to Iraq in January 2008 with a Marine infantry battalion. At that time there was an ongoing debate in America about whether President Bush's "surge" in Iraq had worked. This second deployment left no doubt in my mind that it had accomplished great change. Not only was Iraq a completely different country from the one I left in 2005 but Iraq would continue to get safer and more secure during our unit's entire deployment. Let me qualify this statement by saying that people could still get killed in Iraq. I was visiting a battalion outpost when a Humvee with three of our Marines drove over an improvised explosive device (IED) outside the compound walls. Our unit lost two excellent warriors but the gunner from the vehicle survived the attack. He was able to tell me that all three of the vehicle's crew had been singing "Amazing Grace" at the very moment the bomb exploded. After the deployment I shared this miracle with the families of the Marines who had died. The families had a very deep faith, and although they would have preferred their sons being alive, they were comforted that their Marines were worshipping as they crossed into eternity.

In 2012 the Navy sent me to the homeland of the Taliban. I served as the chaplain to a Special Operation Task Force in the south-eastern region of Afghanistan. It was a joint command including Army and Navy special warfare units. The goal of this command was to wage and win a war of counter-insurgency by extending the influence of the central government of Afghanistan. The instrument for accomplishing this strategy was a network of two dozen small outposts. Despite the skill and effectiveness of our American operators in close combat, their mission at each of the village outposts was to support local Afghan forces to do the brunt of the fighting. These tiny bastions of counter-insurgency were usually located in remote areas along known insurgent infiltration routes.

The most memorable visit I made to a village outpost started when our helicopter was waved off due to a mortar attack. Only later did we learn it was "outgoing" fire (meaning American forces were doing the shooting). Eventually our helicopter was able to land as the patrol that needed the artillery support came back inside the wire. Several IED's had been used against the sailors but everyone survived. One of the warriors suggested their survival was due to luck. I said that they should thank God instead. The other warriors must have agreed with me. During the next ten days my assistant and I had the best attendance at Christian services for our entire time in Afghanistan. Participation was even better than the services we held at our main camp that was staffed with hundreds of people.

After I got back from Afghanistan I finished the PhD that I had been working on since before my first deployment. The foundational question of the dissertation was whether the world-wide Church needed a new response for warriors returning home with Posttraumatic Stress Injury (PTSI). In the clinical world the official name for symptoms of traumatic stress that persist longer than 30 days after a traumatic event is Post-Traumatic Stress Disorder (PTSD). I am part of the care-giving community that objects to the word "disorder" as an appropriate term for what is a wound. Due to this objection, and as an attempt to change the popular label for this injury, whenever it is appropriate the term Posttraumatic Stress Injury and PTSI will be used instead of PTSD in the narrative of this book. When clinical trials or official documents are referenced by me, the original wording may have been retained for academic integrity. At the end of this book the citations and bibliography will use the original spelling and/or terminology.

Since most veterans with traumatic stress injury use the Veterans Administration healthcare system, I have adopted the VA spelling for "Posttraumatic" rather than the APA spelling "Post-Traumatic."

My inquiry into the spiritual aspect of PTSI was driven by my own post-deployment experiences. Starting with the LA riots and continuing through my time in Afghanistan, each of my own homecomings has been accompanied by the stress reactions I carried back with me. The most troubling reaction was that I felt there was a barrier between me and God, and between me and my fellow man. None of the answers the Christian community offered seemed to be appropriate for my dislocation. Either I was directed: 1) to perform some activity that looked like repentance for my participation in war; or 2) to seek the answer from secular clinical processes. The flaw in the first response was that I did not sin by answering the call to war nor had I trespassed beyond the limits God set for me while doing my duties. The flaw in the second course was that these clinical processes examine the mind while ignoring my spirit. I knew that God's way, when I found it, would restore me without condemnation since he was the one who had called me to make war. I also knew that God's restoration would happen at the deepest levels of my spirit. With God's help I eventually found his plan in the pages of the Bible. This book contains the results of my research.

2
JESUS AND WARRIORS

The first chaplain mentioned in the Bible is a priest named Melchizedek. In Genesis 14 he blesses a group of veterans coming home from war. When this encounter is retold in the New Testament their reintegration is described as ". . . returning from the slaughter".[1] Early Christians had to be taught that Melchizedek and his service to returning warriors was the basis for Jesus' heavenly priesthood: "On our behalf Jesus, who has the same type of ordination as Melchizedek, has gone in to Heaven's Temple as the High Priest."[2] I was like these early Christians and was ignorant of the full connection between Jesus and Melchizedek. Until my search for Biblical examples of traumatic stress I did not realize that God chose the first military chaplain to be the model for his Son's ministry. When God opened my mind to this fact I learned something else- that warriors, as warriors, are important to God's work on earth. This new understanding gave me eyes to see in other passages, like the encounter with the Roman Centurion, how Jesus wanted his Church to learn from warriors what it means to make Jesus their Lord.[3]

The Bible tells us that there is nothing new under the sun. Accordingly, I am not the first to see the sacredness of the martial calling. In 1526 Martin Luther wrote a pamphlet called *Whether Soldiers, too, Can Be Saved.* His title suggests that Luther encountered this question many times as a pastor. As he set out the parameters for his response Luther made a distinction between the office of warrior and the person who might hold this position. This disclaimer allowed Luther to set aside the distractions that arise from anecdotal accounts of soldiers who abused the privileges of their vocation. To Luther a rogue serving in the military did not invalidate, by his or her crimes, the divine nature of warrior ministry in the Church. Luther described military service in this way, "...The office of the sword is in itself right and is a divine and useful ordinance, which God does not want us to despise, but to fear, honor, and obey, under penalty of punishment, as St. Paul says in Romans 13 [:1-5]..." He further absolved the warrior of personal responsibility for the carnage of war, "because the hand that wields this sword and kills with it is not man's hand, but God's."[4]

At the start of the New Covenant John the Baptist was asked a question similar to Martin Luther. John's instructions to those in the military were, "Do not use violence to commit extortion or blackmail. And be content with your wages."[5] I know from my own deployments to foreign lands how tempting it is to use the coercive power of deadly force to go beyond what the mission requires. John was asking soldiers to rein themselves in even as Jesus taught civilians who find themselves under martial law to "go the extra mile" when compelled by the military.[6]

The New Testament assumes the reader has a familiarity with the exercises soldiers use for physical fitness and practicing martial arts. Such activities are used to emphasize facts about the soul.[7] Conversely modern Christian warriors would do well to heed the admonition that physical conditioning is of little value without spiritual conditioning.[8] To illustrate how faith can be manifested by the followers of Jesus Christ the Holy Spirit reminds the Church about the warriors who practiced their martial ministry in ancient times:

> What else can I say? There isn't enough time to tell about Gideon, Barak, Samson, Jephthah, David, Samuel, and the prophets. Their faith helped them conquer kingdoms, and because they did right, God made promises to them. They closed the jaws of lions and put out raging fires and escaped from the swords of their enemies. Although they were weak, they were given the strength and power to chase foreign armies away. Some women received their loved ones back from death. Many of these people were tortured, but they refused to be released. They were sure that they would get a better reward when the dead are raised to life. (Heb 11:32-35 CEV).

I draw attention to this recapitulation of Israel's ancient history not to suggest the superiority of warriors' faith but to reiterate the validity of their ministry as warriors under the New Covenant.

Warriors as Priests

It is a Biblical truth that God controls whether a person lives or dies.[9] Thus to take a human life is to enter the realm of the Divine. Under the Old Testament a warrior who used his sword according to the precepts of God was involved in a transaction between Creator and creature every bit as holy as the ministry of the priest in the Temple. This is reflected in the way the Torah describes the total destruction of enemy nations by Moses and Joshua. Prior to each campaign the enemy is "consecrated" (חרם) to God.[10] This is the same word which means, in the context of the altar in the Tabernacle, "an absolute unredeemable grant to God."[11] I have never met a person who completed this "sacrament" that was not transformed by the experience. Whether for good or evil, after a life is extinguished the surviving participant is altered forever. I am **not** saying that every killing is holy or brings glory to God. The Bible teaches that there are occasions when deadly force is a sin[12] and other times when this extreme measure is the only way to please God.[13] My proposition is that there are standards that God has set on a warrior's use of deadly force and, when these conditions are met, this sacrament is as holy as feeding the poor or visiting the sick.

In the New Testament, the authority to practice the sacrament of deadly force is given to the government.[14] In verse four of Romans 13 the text is explicit that the sacramental use of the sword (the basic weapon of law enforcement and military personnel in Roman times) is for punishing evil-doers. This license is a central pillar for Christians who advocate the Just War theory. However, verse one of Romans 13 contains another less explicit, and rarely cited, sanction to transact with God in the sacrament of the sword. This authorization is based on the affirmation that God establishes every government on earth. The apostle Paul used this truth as part of his appeal to the Athenians to embrace the Gospel.[15] He drew the Athenians' attention to the fact that national boundaries change according to God's plans and the seasons he has ordained. No Athenian who knew their city's history had to be told that killing one's enemies in war was the method used for changing national boundaries. The new information Paul provided to these denizens of the city named for Athena, a warrior goddess, was that the Christian God is the one who controls the outcome of war. Paul revealed to them that God's purpose in changing national boundaries and governments is to give people the opportunity to draw close to Him. This is still the basis of the sword sacrament today and does not imply that God is on the side of one army or another. As Abraham Lincoln noted in his Second Inaugural Address, both sides of the conflict prayed to God but neither army had their prayers fully answered. Instead God's will prevailed.[16] His speech suggests that Lincoln had experienced for himself what the patriarch Joshua learned before the fall of Jericho.[17]

The final book of the Christian Bible describes the end of planet Earth in a war to end all wars. This global conflict is the fulfillment of Jesus' prophecy about the Gospel and the sword.[18] Jesus did not participate in sword ministry during his sojourn on earth. He also did not allow the apostles to engage in sword ministry at inappropriate times.[19] Jesus knew, and knows, that the season for his sword ministry is at his Second Coming. When this season comes for Jesus, weapon and warrior are joined in a manner that is inconceivable to our human minds.[20] Until that day, the people who God has called to participate in sword ministry will have to offer their priesthood of war to the best of their abilities and according to the will of God.

Thank You for Your Service

The Catechism of the Catholic Church says, ""The fifth commandment forbids the intentional destruction of human life. Because of the evils and injustices that accompany all war, the Church insistently urges everyone to prayer and to action so that the divine Goodness may free us from the ancient bondage of war."[21] The United Methodist Church's *Social Principles* moves the rejection of war from Mount Sinai to the Gospels: "We believe war is incompatible with the teachings and example of Christ."[22] Although not as explicitly stated as these two examples from mainline denominations, there is a plethora of ministries and liturgies in non-denominational churches that lead warriors to ask forgiveness for their actions during deployment. Similar to *The Catechism* and *The Social Principles* these "services" also send the message that war is a sin. If in fact these denominations and non-denominational church organizations are correct that participation in war is an act that offends God and requires warriors to repent after their homecoming, American Christians need to quit saying to veterans, "Thank you for your service." What other group do we thank when they sin?

On the other hand, if war-fighting is not a sin and American Christians truly are thankful for the service of our men and women, veterans need more from their local church than silent acquiescence that military duty includes killing other human beings. The incredibly transformative act of taking a life should be among the many possible milestones that the universal Church recognizes in a Christian's journey. A warrior who has taken a human life needs to know whether he or she is "Cain" or "Moses" in the eyes of God. Both of these Biblical characters participated in the sacrament of taking a human life and both were marked by God. Cain murdered his brother and was cut off from God's presence. Cain was marked by God to spare him from capital punishment so that his homeless wanderings would be prolonged.[23] In contrast Moses started his ministry to free the Hebrews by killing an Egyptian oppressor.[24] On another occasion Moses was among the consecrated priests who used their swords to kill 3,000 worshipers of the golden calf.[25] This act did not separate him from God, but rather Moses was blessed for it. Following this event, when Moses would spend time in God's presence, his face would glow to the point where it had to be veiled.[26] Given the spiritual nature of taking a human life, I believe the question must be asked: Should not the Church offer a way for people who have participated in the sacrament of the sword to know whether their act was accepted by God or not?

Lot or Legion

Before there was Hiroshima there was the destruction of Sodom and Gomorrah.[27] Abraham's nephew Lot was one of three survivors. Lot also survived an earlier war as a POW.[28] Like the other veterans of the Siddim campaign Lot participated in the first returning-warrior ritual instituted by Melchizedek.[29] Unfortunately for Lot, he needed more than a blessing from his spiritual leader. Lot was overwhelmed by the shadow of death but the soul-cleansing ritual for this wound had not yet been given to human kind. As a result Lot and his family spiraled into all the dysfunctions of PTSI. Many of today's veterans can relate with Lot. They have been exposed to death and are overwhelmed. And like Lot, the spiritual remedies they have been offered have not worked.

During his terrestrial life Jesus was accosted by a man with PTSI outside the village of Gadara. The man identified himself using a military designation. He told Jesus, "My name is Legion."[30] This man was so overshadowed by death that he made his home in the tombs.[31] Besides always thinking about death, the tomb-man of Gadara showed other symptoms of PTSI. He stayed in "fight or flight mode."[32] The tomb-man had trouble sleeping and his coping mechanism was to self-medicate in destructive ways.[33] The tomb-man thought God was his enemy.[34] His spirit was unclean.[35] Jesus addressed all of this veteran's issues and made it possible for him to go home again. America has a multitude of veterans like the tomb-man of Gadara. These men and women have served their country and returned from deployment overshadowed by their exposure to death. All they want is to be able to leave the "tombs" and be re-united to their family and their faith.

CHAPTER 2 ENDNOTES

[1] Heb 7:1 KJV

[2] Heb 6:20 AT

[3] Mt 8:9-10

[4] Martin Luther, "Whether Soldiers, Too, Can Be Saved" in *Luther's Works: The Christian In Society,* vol. 46, edited by Robert C. Schultz, 96

[5] Lk 3:14 AT

[6] Mt 5:41

[7] 1Co 9:26

[8] 1Tm 4:8

[9] Mt 10:29

[10] Num 21:3

[11] Lev 27:29. *Strong's Concordance* s.v. חֵרֶם

[12] Ex 22:3

[13] 1Sam 15:2-3

[14] Rom 13:1-4

[15] Act 17:26

[16] Lincoln's *Second Inaugural Address* is included as an appendix to this book.

[17] Jos 5:13-14

[18] Mt 10:34, Rev 19:19

[19] Mt 26:52-54

[20] Rev 19:21

[21] *Catechism of the Catholic Church,* 2nd ed. 615

[22] *Methodist Social Principles* 165VI.C   http://umc-gbcs.org/social-principles/165-vi.-the-world-community

[23] Gen 4:15

[24] Ex 2:12

[25] Ex 32:28-29

[26] Ex 34:29

[27] Gen 19:24-25

[28] Gen 14:12

[29] Gen 14:18-20

[30] Mk 5:9

[31] Mk 5:3; Lk 8:27

[32] Mk 5:4

[33] Mk 5:5

[34] Mk 5:7

[35] Mk 5:2

3
DEATH-SHADOW

Not everyone who puts on a uniform is called to offer the sacrament of the sword. In the wars of the last fifty years most U.S. personnel never fired their weapon at an enemy. But millions of those warriors did deploy to places where their own death was an ever-present possibility. Jesus said, ". . . for everyone that draws a weapon will die because of it."[1] His words carry an echo of God's warning to Adam, "but of the tree of the knowledge of good and evil you shall not eat, for in the day that you eat of it you shall surely die."[2] Christians know the rest of the story: Adam's body did not die on the day he ate from the tree but his soul was marked for death. In a similar vein Jesus' warning to warriors is: Even those who survive their deployment will come home carrying the shadow of death.

The American Psychiatric Association lists exposure to a deadly environment as the first requirement for Post-Traumatic Stress Disorder (PTSD).[3] Posttraumatic stress is the most common wound found in veterans of Operation Enduring Freedom (OEF) and Operation Iraqi Freedom (OIF).[4] God told the Israelites that exposure to a deadly environment would affect their relationship with him and with their community. Here are his instructions:

> Whoever touches the dead body of any person, and does not purify himself or herself, defiles the tabernacle of God and that soul shall be cut off from Israel. Because the water of purification was not sprinkled upon the living person, this person shall be unclean as long as he or she lives.

> This is the law when a man or woman dies in a dwelling place. All that come into that space, and everything in the building, shall be unclean seven days. . . And whoever is outdoors when he or she touches a person that was killed by violence, or discovers a dead

body, or a human bone, or a grave, shall be unclean seven days. And for the unclean the minister shall take of the cleansing ashes of the burnt heifer, and mix it with running water in a vessel. And this clean person shall take hyssop and dip in the mixture, and sprinkle upon the dwelling and upon all the vessels, and upon the persons that were there, and upon the person that touched a bone, or someone killed, or someone dead, or a grave. (Num 19:13-18 AT)

The diagnosis of PTSI was not even possible prior to 1980.[5] Scholars acknowledge that the disorder currently called PTSI has had many names through the history of war.[6] William Nash, one of the foremost authorities on psychological injuries from the War on Terror, says, "Persistent reactions to combat and operational stress are clearly identifiable in the literature of antiquity."[7] The Greek historian Herodotus, in the fifth century B.C., labeled one man with symptoms of warzone stress "the Trembler."[8] In the 1600's "Swiss Disease" was the name given by other nations to the aberrant behavior of many Swiss conscripts in foreign armies after their first taste of combat.[9] When this malady was shown to affect other nationalities, it was renamed "nostalgia."[10] The first purely American moniker for battle-related psychological breakdown arose during the Civil War when doctors began diagnosing "soldier's heart."[11] World War I veterans called this unseen plague "shell-shock", and the World War II generation labeled it "battle fatigue."[12] Only after the Vietnam War did clinicians start calling the emotional and psychological injuries of combat Post-Traumatic Stress [Injury].

The Old Testament Hebrew word for PTSI is צלמות (tsalmaveth). This term is introduced into Scripture by Job, who suffered from this psychological wound after a guerrilla attack on his property.[13] Just like a modern veteran diagnosed with PTSI, Job had four clinical markers required by the American Psychiatric Association: 1) Exposure to a deadly environment; 2) Re-experiencing the trauma- e.g. flashbacks and intrusive thoughts;[14] 3) Numbing and avoidance- e.g. shrinking from situations that trigger memory;[15] and 4) Hyper arousal- i.e. the inability to sleep and extreme vigilance.[16] For Job these unwanted aspects of his soul grew in the dark of צלמות. This Hebrew word is translated as "shadow of death" in *Strong's Concordance* and older English versions of the Bible.[17] Because of the poetic and traditional associations with "shadow of death" I have chosen to translate צלמות as the compound word "death-shadow" to reflect the actual Hebrew root and to better describe what happened to Job as a participant in war. Besides Job, the warrior King David also used צלמות to describe symptoms akin to modern manifestations of PTSI.

In three psalms (Psalm 23, 44 and 107) David explored the way צלמות (death-shadow) changes a person's life. In Psalm 107 his focus is on the "redeemed." One characteristic of their "redemption" is survival on the battlefield (v. 2). David uses "death-shadow" (צלמות) to describe how these former warriors experienced depression and homelessness (v. 4 and 10). He even recognized "death-shadow" in the sailors of Ancient Israel who did not face enemy fire, but encountered their exposure to death in a hurricane (v. 23-26). In Psalm 44, written to a particular military unit (the Benim Korah), "death-shadow" is accompanied by rejection from their fellow countrymen for service in an exotic land (v.13 and 19). These verses show that Vietnam vets were not the first warriors to have a rough homecoming. The best known psalm in the Bible, Psalm 23, contains David's own struggle with PTSI and how God sustained him through it.

The prophet Isaiah lived during the time when PTSI was healed in Israel according to the quarantine described in Numbers 31 and the wash set forth in Numbers 19. God revealed to Isaiah the eventual cure to death-shadow by a completely different agency: "The people who walked in darkness have seen a great light; a spotlight illuminates they who dwell in the land of death-shadow (צלמות)."[18] Churches around the world read Isaiah's prophecy at Christmas time because it speaks of the birth of the Prince of Peace.[19] The four verses before the Child's arrival describe a situation very different from the Christmas season:

> The people who walked in darkness have seen a great light; a spotlight illuminates they who dwell in the land of death-shadow (צלמות), . . . They rejoice before You according to the joy of

harvest-time, and as men rejoice when they divide the spoils of war. For You have broken the shackles of their forced labor and the baton used on their back and the whip of their taskmaster, just like You did when the Midianites occupied Israel. The people will shake off their dirty boots, and burn their bloody clothes because a Child has been born to us . . . and the expansion of his government and of peace will never end. (Isa 9:2-7 AT)

Isaiah's Ninth chapter paints a picture like America's celebration at the end of World War II. Jesus' incarnation is meant to heal and to free a war-weary nation full of people enslaved by the fear of death. The Holy Spirit revealed to Isaiah that the One who would come as a human child is God's answer to the spiritual separation caused by exposure to war and other deadly situations.

CHAPTER 3 ENDNOTES

[1] Mt 26:52 AT

[2] Gen 2:17

[3] American Psychiatric Association, *Diagnostic and Statistical Manual of Mental Disorders, 4th ed., text rev.*, 463

[4] Dakota J. Kaiser, "Combat Related Post Traumatic Stress Disorder in Veterans of Operation Enduring Freedom and Operation Iraqi Freedom: A Review of the Literature", *Graduate Journal of Counseling Psychology*, Vol 3, no. 1 http://epublications.marquette.edu/gjcp/vol3/iss1/5

[5] William P. Nash, "Combat/Operational Stress Adaptations and Injuries," in *Combat Stress Injury*, 38.

[6] Charles Slack, "PTSD Timeline: Centuries of Trauma," *Protomag* http://protomag.com/assets/ptsd-timeline-centuries-of-trauma

[7] William P. Nash, "Combat/Operational Stress Adaptations and Injuries," in *Combat Stress Injury,* 33.

[8] Charles Slack, "PTSD Timeline: Centuries of Trauma."

[9] Brett A. Moore and Craig M Reger, "Historical and Contemporary Perspectives of Combat Stress and the Army Combat Stress Control Team," in *Combat Stress Injury*, 163

[10] Ibid.

[11] Ibid.

[12] Ibid.

[13] Job 1:15

[14] Job 16:7-19

[15] Job 3:11-25

[16] Job 7:4, 13-14

[17] *Strong's Concordance* s.v. צלמות

[18] Isa 9:2 AT

[19] Isa 9:6

4
THE USUAL SUSPECTS

Job's friends were convinced that Job's suffering was caused by a moral infraction. Similarly many in today's therapeutic community use the term "moral injury" to link violating one's conscience with the onset of PTSI.[1] Although most Christian laity do not use clinical terminology, the majority of believers who talk to me concerning PTSI agree with clinicians that the spiritual core of war-related PTSI is participation in an event beyond civilian peacetime morality. These believers have a deep respect for the military, yet they are unable to recognize how much they sound like Job's friends. In any other situation they would describe participation in an event outside the bounds of decent behavior (civilian peacetime morality) as "sin".

The trend towards a sin-oriented response to veteran re-integration began very early in the Church. Bernard J. Verkamp writes in *The Moral Treatment of Returning Warriors in Early Medieval and Modern Times* that, "[T]here evolved out of the notion of cultic purity a sense of inward purity of the heart . .. Impurity, in other words, was transferred inward and came to be associated with sin."[2] The rejection of warfare, as violating the 5th commandment and possibly the New Testament restriction against "blood"[3], is considered by most scholars to have been standard practice in the early church.[4] Some of the first leaders, such as Tertullian and Origen, considered blood-guilt to be an "irremissable" sin, and thus beyond the reach of human agency.[5] Tertullian was not just concerned with those who engaged in combat. Citing the conflict between vows to the state and the inner loyalty required of a Christian to Jesus alone, Tertullian viewed every aspect of military service, including guard duty, as sin.[6]

The climate of pacifism in the early Church was undone by the battle of the Milvian Bridge in 312 A.D.[7] Legend has it that the Roman Emperor Constantine received a vision that showed him a cross and told him, "by this sign conquer."[8] Constantine's embrace of Christianity altered the structure of military service in the Roman Empire. Soldiers no longer were required to participate in pagan rituals that deified the emperor instead of Christ. The termination of this practice removed a major impediment for Christians to serve in Roman Legions.[9] In fact, by 416 A.D. only Christians could serve in the Roman military.[10] Although the increase in enlistments changed the public's perception of Christians in the military, it was the writings of Augustine of Hippo that changed the Church's theology about war.[11]

According to Augustine, the "wise man" (meaning "Christian") had a duty to wage war to resist injustice.[12] Done as a duty, it was morally neutral, and did not need purification.[13] But this duty did not give Christians license to fight in a manner that was immoral or evil.[14] It was not the outward act for Augustine that constituted the uncleanness, but a person's inner attitude.[15] Augustine, building on the earlier works of many philosophers and theologians, enumerated the conditions that legitimized military action by the state: 1) War must have a just cause; 2) War must be declared by rightful authority; 3) War must be waged with right intention.[16] Those conditions are referred to, in modern parlance, as the Just War Theory.[17] The Latin word used by Augustine for his first condition is "jus." This Latin word means "just" in the sense of "right" and "legal." By establishing a juridical standard for the conduct of war, Augustine eliminated the death pollution of the Mosaic code (Num 19 and 31) as a possible outcome from war. Augustine's use of a legal paradigm also set in motion the idea of restitution by the guilty party. As one modern scholar comments "Plain justice demands that we right the wrongs that we do to the best of our ability."[18] In the early and medieval Church this was manifested in the practice of sin purification known as penance.[19]

With the development of "penance", Bernard Verkamp believes the Christian Church had found a substitute for cleansing veterans with "the ashes of a heifer" prescribed in Numbers 19 and carried out in Numbers 31.[20] Darrell Clay, in his article, "Just War, Penance and the Church" agrees with Verkamp's connection between Numbers 31 and penance. Both authors try to relate the institution of penance with *horror sanguinis*, the primeval superstition associated with shedding blood, but eventually concede that penance had less to do with cultic purity than atoning for guilt.[21] Clay endorses the tradition and practice of penance for today's military veterans, "Should the church fail to discipline one who has violated the moral order, further violations may result. This is especially true in warfare, which is brutal enough as it is and very susceptible to progressive immorality. The church has to be the church, so its members cannot live viciously."[22] This insight into Clay's thinking confirms that penance does not address the death-pollution issue at stake in Numbers 31, nor does "violate the moral order" or "viciously" explain the ritual required by Moses. In chapter 31 everyone returning from war is washed with the ashes of the red heifer including the captives. Nothing in the Hebrew text suggests that adolescent female virgin prisoners-of-war were "vicious" or had "violated the moral order." Yet these girls had to undergo the same purification as the warriors who had slain the girls' fathers and brothers.[23]

The Church's earliest attempt to levy penance on veterans was by withholding the elements of the communion table. In the fourth century Basil the Great recommended that warriors who had shed blood, "abstain from communion for three years."[24] In the centuries that followed a genre of instructive manuals for penance developed called "penitentials."[25] Initially these writings equated slaying enemy soldiers on the battlefield with homicide, but by the late seventh century a distinction was made for soldiers who killed at the command of their leader or "in a public war."[26] The standard purification process for these guilty warriors was 40 days of fasting and humiliation.[27] Not only did penance absolve the guilt from the warrior but, through these exercises, penance also allowed the veteran to "recover the favor of God."[28]

No longer officially called the Sacrament of Penance, the Roman Catholic Church still offers a form of sin purification that would grant absolution from blood-guilt to veterans. The modern name of this ministry is the Sacrament of Reconciliation. The two components or "signs" of the sacrament confirm that Reconciliation primarily targets "moral transgression." The two "signs" are the participant's sorrow for their actions (in this case the warrior's deeds while on deployment) and the priest's words of absolution. "The church teaches that when we perform these outward signs, our sins are washed away, and we are made right with God once more."[29] Although Protestants initially shared some of the same ideas about penance[30], the consensus of most non-Catholics changed after the Enlightenment, and Protestants have largely discontinued the practice of ecclesiastical authorities imposing temporal sanctions in the context of absolution.[31]

The Other Side of the Wittenberg Door

Modern Protestants may lack the concept of "penance" but there are Protestant versions of sin-purification ministries directed towards warriors with PTSI. Sometimes the moral transgression is assigned to enemy soldiers because the foe's guilt is said to have repercussions for American veterans. For example, Military Ministry counselor Chris Adsit tells the wife of a wounded warrior, "Your husband's condition is due to the sinful actions of men – not God."[32] Adsit does not call the veteran with PTSI a sinner, but does assign the root of this malady to rebellion against God. Adsit's how-to book for returning warriors, *The Combat Trauma Healing Manual: Christ-centered Solutions for Combat Trauma* (endorsed by Military Ministry and large networks of Protestant churches) contains "exercises" that are sin-purification rituals in all but name. The simplest is an exercise called "spiritual breathing." The first step to "exhale" is confessing personal sins (p.39). The *Manual* deepens the metaphorical use of respiration with the illustration of a drowning man expelling the water in his lungs. The contamination of past actions progresses in Adsit's symbolism from a harmful gas to a substance that actually blocks the veteran from receiving what he or she needs to live. Learning to "spiritually breathe" removes those impurities and is recommended, "As often as you need to . . . once a week, once a day, once an hour or even once every few minutes!" (p.39).

Another form of purging recommended by Military Ministry is journaling. Adsit suggests that veterans write down as much as they can remember of the incident at the root of their trauma. Instead of "respiration," Adsit uses technical and tactile images to represent the moral pollution caused by war. Journaling helps veterans own the memories they have been hiding in their subconscious that are like a "computer virus" or "splinter in your finger" (p.53). By completing the journal entries these foreign objects at the root of the veteran's PTSI will be ejected (p.53).

Quoting David Grossman, an expert on the effects of combat, Adsit assures his readers, "You're only as sick as your secrets" (p.53). If journaling is not sufficient, then the *Manual* offers a "Memorial Project." This rite also starts off with a written confession as the veteran makes a list of his or her sins and puts it in a jar (p.82). The list is burned and the jar is then sealed. It is a "memorial" to God's forgiveness of confessed sin which allows the veteran to declare, "I am clean before God" (p.83).

Elim Lutheran Church of Blackhoof, Minnesota established their veterans ministry based on the book *Welcome Them Home Help Them Heal*.[33] This publication is recommended by the Department of Defense as a resource for PTSI. The first step of the "Transition from Soldier to Citizen," which is the title of the book's second chapter, is "shedding" elements from the combat zone (p.22). The detritus to be purged are the psychological aspects of military conditioning that prevent safe re-integration to civilian society. In the context of the chapter it is clear that "shedding" is a euphemism setting the stage for later purification exercises. According to *Welcome Them Home*, a wide spectrum of behaviors, thought processes, and experiences must be "shed" or purged from the returning warrior. In these early pages of the book the sin basis of the purification is not mentioned. Only as spiritual topics surface does "shedding" become fixated on the violations of conscience the warrior experienced (p.27). The book states, "In the Christian tradition, war has long been regarded as a gross consequence of human failure" (p.42). In order to deal with the assumed moral outrages at the root of their PTSI veterans are encouraged to create a lamentation. This is defined as "a personal poem of pain and grief" (p.46). Although this exercise does not require a confession, the bullet points provided in *Welcome* offer guilt and shame as possible material for the lament. The rite concludes with the analogy that "our broken relationship with God and each other [is] symbolized graphically in the images of war" (p.46).

After the veteran has lamented, he or she is directed to tell their "story," which may contain "pronounced guilt and shame" (p.50). *Welcome Them Home* warns church members who are part of the "story" process that, "Veterans seeking forgiveness and reconciliation after war-related trauma bear heavy burdens... When a veteran delves into confessional material ... listeners need to be prepared for disturbing accounts and intense emotional release" (p.70). Church members are warned that this unburdening may lead the veteran to ask for a formal purification rite like Confession and Reconciliation (p.71). The book advocates a series of rituals that churches should provide to veterans throughout the liturgical year and offers a prototype called the "Advent Heart-Cleansing Ritual." This rite builds up to a confessional prayer and a symbolic purging by burning slips of paper containing past emotional wounds (p.81). Its purpose is "identifying and letting go of obstacles that separate us from God and from one another" (p.80). *Welcome* recommends for churches to conduct this ceremony at the start of Advent in either November or December and repeat it at Lent (p.82).

Other Protestant veterans' ministries that focus on sin-purification to alleviate PTSI encourage ministers to be a surrogate and declare the sins of the warrior. Operation Barnabas utilizes the liturgical leader to confess, "Where our brothers and sisters in uniform have stumbled and done that which is not pleasing in your sight, grant your rich Word of forgiveness."[34] The Presbyterian Church, U.S.A. instructs their worship leaders to anticipate guilt "haunting many returning veterans" and to construct appropriate "public confession" to absolve the warriors of their culpability.[35] The United Methodist Church utilizes the minister to suggest that the assembled veterans may have acted ". . . outside the parameters of civilized behavior."[36] The Methodist liturgy then allows a few moments of silence for the warriors to be more specific in their confession to God before the minister gives the assurance of pardon. These are just three examples of surrogate confession rites but countless other variations are in use throughout Christianity. In the eyes of the Church sometimes even chaplains are guilty for their military service. In an article by the United Methodist News Service, the reporter began her story about a group of military chaplains with the words, "In the name of Jesus Christ you are forgiven."[37]

Just as Job's friends were wrong to diagnose his death-shadow as the result of immorality, so too are ministries that respond to PTSI using sin-based solutions. The *Diagnostic and Statistical Manual* and Numbers 19 demonstrate that the root of PTSI/death-shadow does not grow out of killing another human-being (blood-guilt) or personally witnessing the horrors of war (moral injury). The root is germinated merely by exposure to a deadly environment without regard to any violation of morality or societal niceties. PTSI/death-shadow is more akin to nuclear radiation which also causes unseen damage to those subjected to its invisible energy. In the same sense that radiation poisoning happens without regard to the person's activities or awareness of their danger, death-shadow is caused by proximity and not culpability. When this exposure-based wound is not dealt with as such, it is rational to expect that, like radiation poisoning, further injury results until decontamination takes place.

CHAPTER 4 ENDNOTES

[1] Litz, Brett T et al., "Moral Injury and Moral Repair: A Preliminary Model and Intervention Strategy." *Clinical Psychology Review* 29, 697.

[2] Bernard J. Verkamp, *The Moral Treatment of Returning Warriors in Early Medieval and Modern Times,* 15.

[3] John Proctor, "Proselytes and Pressure Cookers: The Meaning and Application of Acts 15:20," *International Review of Mission,* 472.

[4] Mark Allman, *Who Would Jesus Kill: War, Peace, and the Christian Tradition,* 77.

[5] John T. McNeill and Helena M. Gamer, *Medieval Handbooks of Penance,* 5.

[6] Tertullian, "On the Crown," Chap 11 quoted in Mark Allman, *Who Would Jesus Kill,* 80.

[7] Roland H. Bainton, *Christian Attitudes Toward War and Peace,* 85.

[8] Ibid. 86.

[9] Mark Allman, *Who Would Jesus Kill,* 83.

[10] Ibid.

[11] Roland H. Bainton, *Christian Attitudes Toward War and Peace,* 99.

[12] Augustine, *City of God,* Book 19, Chap 7, quoted in Mark Allman, *Who Would Jesus Kill,* 171.

[13] Darrell Cole, "Just War, Penance and the Church" *Pro Ecclesia* 11 no. 3, 316.

[14] Roland H. Bainton, *Christian Attitudes Toward War and Peace,* 97.

[15] Ibid. 92.

[16] Mark Allman, *Who Would Jesus Kill,* 167-168.

[17] Louis V. Iasiello, *Jus in Bellum: Key Issues for a Contemporary Assessment of Just Behavior in War,* (PhD diss.), 10.

[18] Darrell Cole, "Just War, Penance and the Church", 327.

[19] Bernard J. Verkamp, *The Moral Treatment of Returning Warriors in Early Medieval and Modern Times,* 23.

[20] Ibid. 10.

[21] Bernard J. Vernkamp, "Moral Treatment of Returning Warriors in the Early Middle Ages," *Journal of Religious Ethics,* 229 and Darrell Cole, *Just War, Penance and the Church,* 319.

[22] Darrell Cole, "Just War, Penance and the Church," 323.

[23] Num 31:19

[24] Quoted in Roland H. Bainton's, *Christian Attitudes Toward War and Peace,* 78.

[25] Mark Allman, *Who Would Jesus Kill*, 171.

[26] Bernard J. Verkamp, *The Moral Treatment of Returning Warriors in Early Medieval and Modern Times*, 2.

[27] John T. McNeill and Helena M. Gamer, *Medieval Handbooks of Penance*, 187, 225, 317.

[28] Ibid. 15.

[29] Leo Zanchettin, ed., "A Sign that Heals," *The Word Among Us*, 5.

[30] Darrell Cole, "Just War, Penance and the Church," *Pro Ecclesia*, 322.

[31] Thomas E. Madden, "Inventing the Crusades," *First Things*, 43.

[32] Chris Adsit, Rahnella Adsit, and Marshele Carter Waddell, *When War Comes Home: Christ-Centered Healing for Wives of Combat Veterans*, 10.

[33] John Sippola et al., *Welcome Them Home Help Them Heal: Pastoral Care and Ministry with Service Members Returning from War*

[34] Operation Barnabas, From the link "Service Of Welcome For A Returning Veteran," http://barnabas.lcmsworldmission.org/?page_id=624

[35] Christopher Dorn and John Zemmler,"The Invisible Wounds of War: Post-Traumatic Stress Disorder and Liturgy in Conversation" in *Call to Worship*, 6.

[36] Laura Bender, "An Order for Welcoming Service Members Returning from War." http://www.gbhem.org/site/apps/nlnet/content2.aspx?c=lsKSL3POLvF&b=5079785&ct=4969667

[37] Kathy L. Gilbert, "Chaplains: Church Must Support Returning Soldiers," *United Methodist News Service*, http://www.umc.org/site/apps/nl/content3.asp?c=lwL4KnN1LtH&b=2429867&ct=3574065

5
THE WARRIOR WASH

In Numbers 31 God decreed that all participants of a military campaign undergo a ritual wash to relieve the spiritual damage caused by death-shadow. This included POW's and other non-combatants. The substance prescribed to wash the veterans was ash-slurry from a red heifer. The process for making and applying this slurry is described in Numbers 19. In Jewish tradition the use of heifer ashes for death-shadow decontamination also requires the participation of priests descended from the patriarch Levi.[1]

The destruction of the Second Temple made it impossible for the sons of Levi to continue their priestly duties. However, this destruction had no effect on Jesus who is a priest at the "greater and more perfect tabernacle, not made with hands."[2] In Hebrews 9:13-14 the Church is told "For if . . . the ashes of a heifer sprinkling the unclean sanctifies to the purifying of the flesh, how much more shall the blood of Christ . . . purge your conscience from works of death[3] to serve the living God?" In other words, under the First Covenant the heifer-ash liquid washed the death-shadow from a person's body. Now in the Final Covenant, the blood of Jesus is the solvent to wash the death-shadow from a person's soul.

Anthropologist Mary Douglas noted "For it is a mistake to suppose that there can be religion which is all interior, with no rules, no liturgy, no external signs of inward states. . . For an external symbol can mysteriously help the coordination of brain and body."[4] Most branches of Christianity recognize the validity of Douglas' observation and include external symbols to proclaim the Gospel. For example, in the rite of Communion, the Church re-enacts Jesus' final meal with his disciples. The structure of the ceremony is driven by the events recorded in Scripture. So too is the rite of baptism a reenactment of a Biblical narrative.[5] The warrior wash for modern veterans is patterned on the rite Moses conducted on the plains of Moab.[6] Biblical scholars have observed that the military version of the death-shadow ritual is heavily dependent on the civilian rite ordained by God in Numbers 19.[7] In both versions of death-shadow decontamination the cleansing took place over a seven day period.[8] The modern adaptation keeps this seven day structure. From the New Testament, the contemporary warrior wash takes the mandate of Hebrews 9 and replaces the ashes of the heifer with the blood of Jesus.[9] In addition to death-shadow there were six other deployment issues that Moses addressed among his veterans. Over three thousand years have passed since the Moabite campaign but these same factors impede today's warriors from gaining closure on their deployment so all six are included in the 21st century adaptation of God's healing camp.

General Orders for Returning Warriors

Starting on the first day of Basic Training and continuing until a service member is discharged or retires, General Orders form the backdrop of American military life. A "General Order" is a command that is binding on all members of a particular service. For example, there was a time when all branches of the U.S. military followed the same 11 General Orders for Sentries and Personnel Standing Watch. In a similar fashion God instituted seven General Orders for returning warriors in Numbers 31. These General Orders are:

1) Establish a decontamination camp.

2) Conduct a muster and account for all personnel.

3) Adjudicate any cases of Conduct Unbecoming of a Leader.

4) Eliminate sexual surrogates.

5) Refute urban legends affecting faith.

6) Divide spoils between veterans and civilians.

7) Cleanse all redeploying personnel of death-shadow.

The Warrior Wash uses these seven General Orders to guide the work of spiritual reintegration from deployment. Since there are seven orders, and the veterans are together seven days, each day of the convocation is focused on a single General Order. To understand God's purpose for each statute there is a presentation to the entire "camp" followed by a small group activity to help participants connect God's instruction to his or her post-deployment life.

General Order #1 Establish Decontamination Camp

The first General Order instructs the Christian community to provide a place for veterans to process the experiences they bring back from war. The returning warriors are not intended to stay in this artificial camp for an extended period but there is work to be done in this transit point that cannot be accomplished while the veterans are still engaged in fighting the war or after they have returned to the concerns of normal life among family and peacetime society.

On the plains of Moab the returning warriors were met by Moses and Eleazar, who themselves were veterans of earlier campaigns. From a sociologist's point of view these two veterans of past wars performed the work of "ritual elders," a common method of establishing sacred time and space.[10] In the modern ceremony the participating warriors also are welcomed by veterans of earlier deployments. The reception of one "generation" by its "ancestors" is a non-verbal expression of continuity, a key ingredient in an effective ceremony.[11] To avoid confusion caused by similarity of terms, the veterans of previous campaigns who are assisting in a warrior wash are called "proctors" rather than "elders." The proctors take on the duties of Moses and Eleazar and facilitate the initial arrival and processing of returning warriors to the cleansing "camp."

Another important function of the proctors is to set the demeanor of the "camp." In the context of death-shadow the proctors' job is to minimize the inter-service rivalry that is common among all veterans' groups. Establishing an environment free of deprecation and put-down humor is counter-intuitive for most veterans. However the practice of exalting one's own branch of service while demeaning other veterans' hinders the work that God wants to do in his returning warriors by maintaining barriers and a sense of "otherness."

Stratification based on rank, number of deployments, or exposure to extreme events can occur when veterans gather together. The proctors must prevent any hierarchy from developing among the wash attendees. The reason leveling is a necessary component of the wash is because death-shadow is no respecter of persons. This wound can tarnish the soul of any warrior who deploys regardless of his or her pay-grade, the number of days spent in-country, and without considering whether a particular veteran was involved in kinetic warfare or the most rear-echelon service support. Experience has shown that unless the proctors set an example of common humility many spiritually wounded warriors will not fully participate in the wash because they feel unworthy of their wounds. General Order #1 is accomplished when the proctors have established an environment where autobiographical stories can be shared in safety.

General Order #2 – Muster the Troops

The second General Order is to conduct a "muster." All branches of the U.S. military use some method to account for their members. Accountability was also a regular feature of military operations in Ancient Israel.[12] Moses had his leaders conduct a muster to see if anyone was lost on the Moab deployment.[13] The purpose of the "muster" in the contemporary ceremony is to allow participating veterans to honor the fallen members of their unit and to symbolically restore the unit to its pre-deployment structure. Failure to acknowledge the power of community still felt by the living for the dead was one of the traumatizing aspects of the Vietnam War.[14]

Since U.S. forces conduct memorial services in the theatre of war for any casualties sustained by a unit, and often a second memorial service is conducted with families present after a unit returns to their home station, the "muster" for General Order #2 is not meant to be another memorial service. Rather it is recognition that in modern warfare warriors killed in action arrive home in a separate process from the living warriors. A two tier evacuation system was not how ancient armies finished a campaign. The living and the dead came home together and this unity provided emotional closure.[15] Taking a cue from primeval homecomings, the contemporary muster is meant to create an environment where the entire unit, both the living and the fallen, are present again as if they came home on the same plane or ship. This re-assembly is done through a symbolic gesture. An illustration of such a gesture is the Doolittle Raiders' Toasting Goblets. Although all but four of the eighty original Raiders have died, the unit is perpetually together in the display case that holds all eighty goblets. The living (4) are represented by goblets that are right-side up, the deceased by goblets that are inverted. Author and retired VA psychologist Dr. Jonathan Shay notes in *Achilles in Vietnam* that there can be a "resuscitative function" in the mental exercises a veteran does to feel like the dead are "present" again.[16]

In Moses' warrior wash, the muster allowed the Israelite veterans to celebrate that they had returned alive. In the modern version the muster is also the time to celebrate individual survival and to address the subject of "survivor's guilt" if it is present in any of the veterans. The manifestation of "survivor's guilt" is an associated feature of PTSI when the traumatic event is experienced by a group.[17] Dr. William Nash, who is a consultant on combat/operational stress control policies and programs for the military and the VA, has noted that many warriors ". . . sometimes condemn themselves for the simple act of returning home alive when others perished."[18] Dr. Shay, a colleague of Dr. Nash, observes in both ancient and modern veterans that guilt is a common reaction to surviving.[19] In the Bible, "survivor's guilt" was one reason for Elijah's depression after the other members of his order perished in a governmental purge.[20] King David also experienced "survivor's guilt" at the end of one campaign.[21] It is noteworthy that Elijah's "survivor's guilt" is the only aspect of his suffering that God sought to comfort in Elijah. God did this by informing Elijah that 7000 other members of his unit had also survived.[22] During the modern warrior wash the proctors are God's voice to proclaim that it is good to survive a time of war, even when others perish.

General Order 3 – Adjudicate Conduct Unbecoming

General Order #3 addresses the wounds caused by "conduct unbecoming of a leader." *The Manual for Courts-Martial* sets the parameters for "Conduct Unbecoming of an Officer" as

> "There are certain moral attributes common to the ideal officer and the perfect gentleman, a lack of which is indicated by acts of dishonesty, unfair dealing, indecency, indecorum, lawlessness, injustice, or cruelty."[23]

Although the U.S. military makes the above infractions a chargeable offense only for commissioned officers, in the spiritual world, all leaders must maintain a higher code of conduct than their subordinates.[24] The men in charge of the Midianite raid committed "conduct unbecoming of a leader" when they pandered to their own sexual desires rather than following God's instructions.[25] Moses let these supervisors know that their unbecoming conduct put the survival of their unit and the entire nation at risk. VA psychiatrist Dr. Shay has determined that both ancient and modern warriors are made vulnerable to PTSI when their leaders fail to do "what's right."[26] Shay notes that when military leaders willfully take advantage of their position ". . . the [human] body codes it in much the same way it codes physical attack."[27]

"Conduct Unbecoming of a Leader" is difficult to address in a group setting because there will always be a mixture of ranks in any veterans' gathering. Senior NCO's (non-commissioned officers) and officers, even if retired, react with defensiveness when this subject is broached. They perceive it as a criticism of their leadership even when no one from their unit is in the group. There is also a tendency for this conversation to quickly deteriorate into a carping session about everything that was negative during a deployment. The proctors of the modern warrior wash must be quick to direct the focus of the veterans' engagement with "Conduct Unbecoming of a Leader" back to the work God wants veterans to do in **themselves**. In simple terms this work is: 1) To acknowledge if they themselves added to the stress of a deadly environment by not being a trustworthy leader; 2) To forgive any person in authority whose decisions or command climate was the cause for bitterness to take root in their soul.

General Order #4 – Eliminate Sexual Surrogates

The fourth General Order in the modern cleansing rite is a separation process for the veterans from illicit sexual relations (sexual surrogates). In Ancient Israel a calamity came upon the entire nation when its fighting men brought home sexual practices they had picked up while on campaign.[28] Even though the army of Israel was victorious over the Midianites without fighting a single battle, the sexual license practiced by the troops brought death to 24,000 of their own people after the deployment.[29] If this account were only mentioned in the Old Testament Christians might be able to dismiss this narrative as a remnant from another age. However, the Midianite campaign's toxic sexual recipe is also condemned in the New Testament at 2 Peter 2:14-15, and thus is highly relevant for Christian warriors. In the context of General Order #4 a "sexual surrogate" is any sexual practice that replaces or distracts the physical intimacy between a man and a woman married to each other.

In the original warrior wash Moses insisted that his veterans be separated from illicit sexual relations represented by some of their foreign captives.[30] The captives that were a threat to Moses' troops advocated sexual relations outside the ordinances of God. The foreign women with no history of illicit sexual relations posed no danger to the Israelite warriors, or to the rest of the nation, and were integrated into civilian society. In a similar manner the threat to America's culture does not come through "war-spouses" of other nationalities that have been brought home from deployment. Instead the sexual pathogens are latent domestic practices that are constrained on U.S. soil but that bloom to rapacious life on foreign shores.

The most pathological sexual surrogate is the environment of pornography accepted among U.S. forces on deployment.[31] The Greek word *porneuo* (πορνεύω) that forms half of the English word "pornography" is also the root word for the injunction against "fornication" in Acts 15:20. Fornication is one of the few laws from the Old Testament still applicable to Christians.[32] According to *Strong's Concordance* πορνεύω means to, ". . .

indulge unlawful lust (of either sex)."[33] Pornography not only impacts a person's ability to connect with God and his or her spouse,[34] but it is also a common addiction among people wounded by PTSI.[35]

Another form of illicit sexual relations is the "deployment sex pact."[36] Under such a "pact" the sexual boundaries of monogamous marriage are loosed while a military member is deployed. The "deployment sex pact " is just the latest catch-phrase for war-time infidelity which has a pedigree all the way back to King David.[37] The New Testament teaches that any sex act spiritually binds one person to another.[38] The result of a "deployment sex pact," or even unplanned adultery during deployment, is the introduction of another person into a marriage bed already struggling with intimacy problems caused by geographic separation.

There are countless other ways that deployed personnel indulge sexual surrogates rather than comply with God's plan for their bodies. In the case of a believer God has a personal stake in each act of sexual intimacy.[39] For this reason God would have the Church provide a way to separate a warrior from pornography and any other sexual impurity. In the setting of a warrior wash, veterans start their emancipation from these surrogates by reflecting on their sexual behavior while deployed. There is then an opportunity for repentance and re-dedication to sexual purity.

General Order #5 – Refute Urban Legends

In our internet age so many "urban legends" (false reports) are circulating that an entire industry has been created to refute these fallacies. Moses and Eliezer had to address an urban legend when they quarantined the Israelite warriors on the plains of Moab. A priest named Balaam had circulated a false report that the people of God could blend the religious practices of foreign gods with their worship of the God of Israel.[40] Balaam's "urban legend" was even around at the time of the New Testament. In 2 Peter 2 the Holy Spirit described Christians who came under its influence, "Turning out of the true way, they have gone wandering in error, after the way of Balaam, the son of Beor . .."[41] As this warning is meant for Christians in all ages, the mission of General Order #5 is to make sure this "urban legend" (and all other incorrect spiritual information and practices) does not make it back into the homes and churches of our veterans.

Since the start of the War on Terror U.S. forces have been deployed to countries where Islam holds sway. In practice this geographic particular has meant that Christian warriors operate in an environment where some commanders, nearly all local allies, and sometimes even chaplains, keep fostering the urban legend that "we all worship the same God."[42] At civic ceremonies in these host nations it is not uncommon for recitations of the Qu'ran and prayers to Allah to be offered over U.S. forces. Such practices are similar to the rites Na'aman the Syrian was exposed to on deployment in Ancient Israel. In 2 Kings 5 General Na'aman, who worshipped the God of Israel, recognized that his job required him to participate in religious practices that honored the god Rimnon. Na'aman asked forgiveness for being at these services.[43] Many modern veterans need God to grant them Na'aman's dispensation.

In the New Testament Balaam's urban-legend is included in a warning about "false prophets" who will introduce "destructive heresies."[44] The meaning of "heresy" is " . . . an opinion, dogma or practice contrary to the truth."[45] In essence "heresy" and "urban legend" mean the same thing. The Old Testament contains several examples of "false prophets" and "heresies" that were part of military deployments. For instance, during the march out of Egypt a priest named Korah attempted to depose Moses and Aaron as the spiritual leaders of Israel and to introduce forbidden practices.[46] In the time of the Judges, one military unit started their own religion under the spiritual direction of a hireling.[47] These two examples illustrate the harm done by "renegade" teachers.

Although forgotten in the 21st century, the original definition of "renegade" was a deserter from the Christian faith. Similar to the military campaigns in the book of Judges, there are "renegade" teachers among our deployed warriors who gain undue influence over their peers. The power of renegade teachers to corrupt the faith of deployed personnel should come as no surprise to Americans back home who realize the isolation of current wars and the huge ratio of troops-to-chaplains. It is impossible to list every type of heretical teaching among the renegades or "Balaams" that arise during U.S. military campaigns. Yet let it be said that the plethora of urban legends that circulates among the troops can instill in our warriors a distrust of organized religion so deep, that for many, it is impossible to return to civilian-led churches after deployment.

As a response to General Order #5 the modern warrior wash includes two activities to counter the effects of "urban legends": 1) An opportunity to offer a prayer like Na'aman's prayer; 2) An opportunity to affirm the God who has revealed Himself as Father, Son and Holy Spirit.

General Order #6 – Share the Spoils of War

In ancient armies the victor received all the spoils. God had to teach his warriors to view spoils differently. In Numbers 31:26-30, the veterans gave half their spoils to the people who stayed behind, and both parts of the community made an offering to God. In the modern ceremony General Order #6 calls for deployed personnel to share the "spoils" with those who were not present.

There is a Biblical correlation between what returning warriors do with their spoils and the relationship returning warriors have with God and their fellow citizens. In the Bible's first war narrative (Gen 14) Abraham gives a tenth of his spoils to the priest Melchizedek. This act of Abraham's post-deployment generosity is also a key element of New Testament theology. Abraham's sharing of spoils with Melchizedek is cited in the Epistle to the Hebrews to support the supremacy of Jesus' priesthood over the Levitical priesthood.[48] In contrast to Abraham's positive example, King Saul failed to follow God's instructions about spoils from the Amalekite campaign and this failure caused God to remove his favor from Saul.[49]

Sharing spoils has a positive effect for both giver and receiver on a purely human level. It connects people of different life experiences and personal histories. Humans have a natural tendency to associate only with others of similar backgrounds (e.g. military service). Having such a predisposition sometimes causes a pathological breakdown in the social horizon of a warrior with PTSI. In Dr. Shay's analysis of *The Iliad*, he calls this trait "Shrinkage of the Social and Moral Horizon."[50] Shay notes that

Achilles begins the *Iliad* connected to the entire Greek army, but after the indignity done to him by King Agamemnon, he withdraws to just " . . . his own troop, the Myrmidons."[51] In a modern parallel, one of Dr. Shay's patients at the VA admitted that his loyalty shrank from his battalion of 850, then to his company of seventy-two, and finally to just the five men of his reconnaissance team.[52] God knows about this isolating tendency in warriors of every generation and his solution to the shrinkage of social horizon is the sharing of spoils.

The "spoils" shared by modern warriors under General Order #6 are not actual items of value taken from the enemy. This practice is largely prohibited under the Geneva Conventions of War and the U.S. Uniform Code of Military Justice. Rather, in the restored warrior wash veterans are asked to consider how they are richer in prestige or character because of their deployment(s), and to think about ways these "spoils" can be shared with the civilian population in their home town. On this subject Dr. Shay concludes "The earliest inventors of democratic politics invented equal citizen honor [between warriors and civilians] . . . as the necessary psychological and social substructure for democracy."[53] The New Testament puts it another way, "But whoever would be great among you must be your servant, and whoever would be first among you must be your slave, even as the Son of Man came not to be served but to serve, and to give his life as a ransom for many."[54] To symbolize this equality and to complete General Order #6 an official from the local community is invited to the closing ceremony of the Warrior Wash. At the designated point in the service the warriors pin their campaign medals on the local official. The giving and receiving of these hard-won war spoils is a very moving experience for all concerned.

General Order #7- Wash the Warriors

Under the Mosaic Law a person polluted by death was washed after being sequestered seven days.[55] The modern ceremony follows this example and makes the "wash" the final step in the process of healing veterans of death-shadow. To fulfill General Order #7 a ceremony is conducted where the warriors come down to the altar and the minister washes their feet. Having "clean" feet sets the stage for reintegration into the life God has in store for each warrior.

It is worth noting that the last ministry Jesus conducted for his disciples was a foot-wash where he told them, "You do not know what I do now, but you shall know hereafter."[56] Jesus was already aware that in a matter of hours his disciples would be tainted by death-shadow because of the swordfight in the Garden of Gethsemane. So in fulfillment of Isaiah's Messianic prophecy on death-shadow Jesus ministered to their feet.[57]

"Foot" cleansing as a prerequisite to God's presence has a long tradition in Scripture. When Moses met God at the burning bush, God commanded Moses to take off his sandals so that he would not bring uncleanness onto holy ground.[58] This sanitizing action revealed that sin is not the only barrier to communing with God. Jesus also taught that the condition of a person's foot could be a barrier between that person and God.[59] Jesus told Simon Peter he would be cut-off if Jesus did not wash his feet.[60] After this admonition Peter and the other disciples received not only a foot wash but the commission to wash feet as a sign of Christian discipleship.[61]

When Moses' veterans were cleansed the Levites sprinkled all personnel using a branch dipped into water containing the ashes of a heifer.[62] The New Testament says that the blood of Jesus has replaced the ashes of this heifer.[63] At the Last Supper Jesus held a cup of wine and told his disciples, ""This is my blood. It is poured out for you, and with it God makes his new agreement."[64] For this reason the warrior wash is performed using a branch to sprinkle the liquid from the cup of the Lord's Supper upon the feet of the veterans. With this act the shadow of death is cleansed from the veterans' soul and they are now free to live life connected to God and to their fellow human beings.

Multiple Deployments

Most World War II veterans were deployed until the war was over. A one-time warrior wash after V-E or V-J Day would have sufficed for their spiritual wounds from death-shadow. The War on Terror has treated its veterans differently. Ten+ years of war has meant multiple deployments to the valley of the shadow of death for many warriors. In certain instances veterans have been discharged from the military and returned to the wars as civilian contractors. A significant number of veterans have returned from one deployment with symptoms of PTSI and received pharmacological treatments prior to being redeployed to another tour in Iraq or Afghanistan. When wars last as long as our current struggle no one who serves his or her country really knows which deployment will be their last.

Clinical professionals have already recognized the need to treat PTSI without waiting for the last deployment. The Church also should not wait for a veteran's last deployment to offer the warrior wash. On the first return to his or her community a warrior should attend the full seven day treatment. After subsequent deployments a second seven day retreat may not be necessary. If a warrior has a firm grasp on the issues at the heart of General Orders #1 through #6, the veteran need only participate in the actual wash ceremony after each return. The washing ritual is the moment when the warrior's submission to Christ's foot-cleansing meets God's promise that his Son's blood will remove the stains of death from a warrior's soul. Once a warrior understands this transaction it does not have to be re-taught each deployment. In a local church that offers this cleansing, the wash for each subsequent exposure to death-shadow could be included in a regular Sunday service in the same way baptisms and church membership have become part of the order of worship.

CHAPTER 5 ENDNOTES

[1] Jacob Neusner, trans., *The Mishnah: The New Translation*, 1015- 1016.

[2] Heb 9:11

[3] Gary Selby translates νεϰρων εργων as "works of death" in "The Meaning and Function of συνείδησις in Hebrews 9 and 10" in *Restoration Quarterly* 28, 147.

[4] Mary Douglas, *Purity and Danger: An Analysis of the Concepts of Purity and Taboo*, 77.

[5] Luk 3:16,18,21; Acts 8:36-38

[6] Num 31:12

[7] David P. Wright, "Purification from Corpse-Contamination in Numbers XXXI 19-24," *Vetus Testamentum*, 214.

[8] Num 19:16; Nu 31:19

[9] Heb 9:13-14

[10] Edward Tick, *War and the Soul*, 62.

[11] Robin Green, *Only Connect*, 5.

[12] 1Sam 14:17

[13] Num 31:49

[14] Jonathan Shay, *Achilles in Vietnam*, 68.

[15] Ibid. 59.

[16] Ibid. 73.

[17] DSM-III, s.v. "Post-Traumatic Stress Disorder," quoted in "The Psychological Effects of Being a Prisoner of War" by American Psychiatric Association, *Human Adaptation to Extreme Stress*, 166.

[18] William P. Nash, "The Stressors of War" in *Combat Stress Injury*, 26.

[19] Jonathan Shay, *Achilles in Vietnam*, 73.

[20] 1Ki 19:14

[21] 2Sam 18:33

[22] 1Ki 19:18

[23] Joint Service Committee on Military Justice, *The Manual for Courts-Martial United States*, Article 133—Conduct Unbecoming an Officer and Gentleman. (2002 edition).

[24] Ja 3:1

[25] Num 31:14-16

[26] Jonathan Shay, *Odysseus in America*, 240.

[27] Jonathan Shay, "Casualties." *Daedalus*, 183

[28] Num 25

[29] Num 25:1-9

[30] Num 31:15-16
[31] Tom Johansmeyer, "Operation Desert Porn," in *Boston Magazine* http://www.bostonmagazine.com/articles/operation_desert_porn/page2
[32] John Proctor, "Proselytes and Pressure-Cookers: The Meaning and Application of Acts 15:20," *International Review of Mission*, 471.
[33] *Strong's Concordance*, s.v. "πορνεύω."
[34] William M. Struthers, *Wired for Intimacy*, 42.
[35] Southern Baptist Convention, "A Biblical Response To Post Traumatic Stress Disorder (PTSD)," http://www.namb.net/chaplaincyresources/
[36] Diana Falzone, "Should Military Marriages Include a 'Deployment Sex Pact'?" Nov 12, 2012 , FoxNews.Com http://www.foxnews.com/opinion/2012/11/26/military-marriages-and-deployment-sex-pact/
[37] 2Sam 11:1-4
[38] 1Cor 6:16
[39] 1 Cor 6:15
[40] Num 25:2 and 31:16
[41] 2Pe 2:15 BBE
[42] Al Arabiya News, "Bush denies he is an 'enemy of Islam'", http://www.alarabiya.net/articles/2007/10/05/39989.html
[43] 2Ki 5:18
[44] 2Pe 2:1
[45] *Merriam-Webster's Collegiate Dictionary*, s.v. "heresy"
[46] Num 16:1
[47] Jdg 18:27-31
[48] Heb 7:6
[49] 1Sam 15:11
[50] Jonathan Shay, *Achilles in Vietnam,* 23.
[51] Ibid. 28.
[52] Ibid. 24.
[53] Jonathan Shay, *Odysseus in America,* 161.
[54] Mt 20:26-28 ESV
[55] Num 19:16
[56] Jn 13:7
[57] Isa 9:2 and 9:5
[58] Ex 3:5
[59] Mk 9:45
[60] Jn 13:8
[61] Jn 13:14-15
[62] Num 19:17-18; Num 31:19
[63] Heb 9:13-14
[64] Luk 22:20 CEV

PART II

6
DAY EIGHT

When the eighth day dawned on the Plains of Moab, the veterans of Ancient Israel faced the first day of the rest of their lives. It started with an apprenticeship in their community. Under the mentorship of tribal elders the returning veterans learned to live out their spiritual transformation in a civilian context. In a similar way, after Jesus removed the death-shadow from the tomb-man of Gadara, he sent the man back to the Ten Cities as a living sermon.[1] This former legionnaire no longer had to compensate for his PTSI by isolating himself and self-medicating. Yet he was in danger of fulfilling Jesus' warning that people prefer to keep their old habits rather than embracing new ones.[2] To grow into the fullness of his new life, the veteran needed the believers in the Ten Cities to teach him how to live without shadows as much as the Ten Cities needed the wonderful news he brought them.

When a modern warrior completes the seven day warrior wash, he or she also returns to "the Ten Cities" on Day Eight. Only now instead of "Ten Cities" there are thousands of local churches waiting to receive returning warriors. Every congregation needs the testimony of warriors who have been set free from death-shadow to remind their members that God is bigger than the effects of war. Similarly veterans need their local church to walk with them as they learn new habits that are free of death-shadow's influence. Just like a person healed of a broken leg takes their first few steps as if the cast was still in place, a veteran healed of death-shadow starts his or her new life by "walking" in their old wounded way. However, through the graces of his or her local church, a former casualty can be taught to stride without any spiritual limitations from their exposure to war.

Moving beyond the limitations of old wounds is the purpose of Day Eight. The next section of this book offers 11 topical studies to start congregations and veterans exploring their roles in the expansion of God's Kingdom.

Lesson 1

Minister of War: How Do I Use My Gift Back Home?

The Bible reveals there are seasons of war and peace in God's plan for the earth.[3] The same is true for individuals. In the local church the challenge for a person with the gift of war is how to use their aptitude during times of peace or when he or she is not deployed.

At one time in Ancient Israel the Temple had 4000 staff who were armed and took turns providing security.[4] These guardians of the congregation served many functions. Their duties included visitor screening, safeguarding high-value articles, and crowd control. Unfortunately most Christians only know of one operation conducted by this group-- the arrest of Jesus. Because of that night the Church has forgotten the necessary service these ministers performed on behalf of God and his people for over a thousand years.

Merriam-Webster's Collegiate Dictionary defines "sanctuary" as "a consecrated place . . . the most sacred part of a religious building . . . a place of refuge and protection."[5] The Temple in Jerusalem was all of these things. It was the job of the Temple's guardians to keep it so. Most modern churches have sanctuaries that fit the first two parts of *Webster's* definition, but lack the real refuge and protection God's house used to offer. This absence is sorely felt by those Christians who minister to people trying to escape from human-trafficking, abusive relationships, or many other situations that require a barrier against pursuit.

The inability to offer sanctuary is not due to a lack of qualified believers. Rather there is an institutional mindset that never considers using the congregation's members for these duties. To be fair, there are a few organizations in at-risk neighborhoods that utilize the martial giftedness of their members. Like their Levite predecessors, these modern day centurions minister through access control, visitor screening, and safeguarding high-value articles. However, such ministries are far from the norm and extreme situations appear to be the only environment where Christians will accept the ministry of protection in their house of worship.

At a time when large numbers of warriors are unemployed, and an equally vast number are seeking purpose for their lives after a decade at war, this first study is intended to challenge veterans and local churches to think outside the box. It is hoped that churches will utilize an untapped skill-set already in their midst for the glory of God.

OLD TESTAMENT LESSON: Neh 4: 15-23 CEV

> Our enemies found out that we knew about their plot against us, but God kept them from doing what they had planned. So we went back to work on the wall. From then on, I let half of the young men work while the other half stood guard. They wore armor and had spears and shields, as well as bows and arrows. The leaders helped the workers who were rebuilding the wall. Everyone who hauled building materials kept one hand free to carry a weapon. Even the workers who were rebuilding the wall strapped on a sword. The worker who was to blow the signal trumpet stayed with me. I told the people and their officials and leaders, "Our work is so spread out, that we are a long way from one another. If you hear the sound of the trumpet, come quickly and gather around me. Our God will help us fight." Every day from dawn to dark, half of the workers rebuilt the walls, while the rest stood guard with their spears. I asked the men in charge and their workers to stay inside Jerusalem and stand guard at night. So they guarded the city at night and worked during the day. I even slept in my work clothes at night; my children, the workers, and the guards slept in theirs as well. And we always kept our weapons close by.

Key Concept: Building God's Kingdom on earth sometimes means defending it against those who would destroy it.

COMMENTARY

When Nehemiah arrived in Jerusalem the believers were vulnerable to any threat. Nehemiah did not bring any soldiers with him to change this situation but he did bring a mindset that allowed the congregation to protect themselves. Even after the people began to rebuild the gates and walls they still felt vulnerable until Nehemiah instituted guard duty. In the hostile environment of their times, it was not enough to build walls in Jerusalem. These structures required armed citizens to defend them. This realization was the spiritual foundation that allowed the work of rebuilding Jerusalem to succeed. Nehemiah blended the tools for masonry with the tools for self-defense. Only after the community was secure did Nehemiah turn his attention to the spiritual development of the people.

QUESTIONS FOR REFLECTION

Why do you think the people of Jerusalem did not take care of their own security needs before the arrival of Nehemiah?

_____

_____

What are the "enemies" to your community? Does your church have someone like Nehemiah in the congregation?

_____

_____

Do you think churches should have actual "defenders" or "protectors" on the premises?

_____

_____

Is there a possibility that a church with a security ministry might feel more like a fort or police station than a place of worship?

_____

_____

Does your church offer any ministries in at-risk areas? Who is responsible for the safety of the volunteers?

_____

_____

What areas of ministry in your church could benefit by the participation of veterans and those trained in armed conflict and/or security procedures?

_____

_____

NEW TESTAMENT LESSON: Rev 12:7-9, 12-13, 17 ESV

Now war arose in heaven, Michael and his angels fighting against the dragon. And the dragon and his angels fought back, but he was defeated, and there was no longer any place for them in heaven. And the great dragon was thrown down, that ancient serpent, who is called the devil and Satan, the deceiver of the whole world--he was thrown down to the earth, and his angels were thrown down with him. . . Therefore, rejoice, O heavens and you who dwell in them! But woe to you, O earth and sea, for the devil has come down to you in great wrath, because he knows that his time is short!" And when the dragon saw that he had been thrown down to the earth, he pursued the woman who had given birth to the male child. . . . . Then the dragon became furious with the woman and went off to make war on the rest of her offspring, on those who keep the commandments of God and hold to the testimony of Jesus.

Key Concept: Even the angels had to secure heaven. After his defeat the one who threatened heaven now threatens God's children on earth.

COMMENTARY

In the Old Testament Satan was able to come into God's presence whenever God summoned the other angels.[6] This passage reveals that eventually the devil posed a threat to the citizens of God's realm so the angels had to defend their city. They ended the conflict by ejecting the devil and his followers. In whatever way the devil was able to threaten heaven he now brings the same peril to every believer on earth. Like the angels in heaven, the local church is where God has placed the resources for believers to cooperate for their mutual defense in this war.

QUESTIONS FOR REFLECTION

Does this passage help you understand any of the spiritual issues of your deployment? Was your war part of the same struggle as the angels? Is human warfare a proxy war for other spiritual forces?

_____

_____

What divine purpose is served by expelling war from heaven to earth?

_____

_____

Do Christians fight alone or are angels still involved in the war against the devil?

_____

_____

Has your church ever been under spiritual attack? How did the people respond? Are military principles useful when this happens?

_____

_____

Was there ever a time when you felt you were part of a spiritual war? If so, what were the circumstances?

_____

_____

In your experience are most believers aware of the war being waged against them?

_____

_____

Based on your deployment experiences, what spiritual habits or practices would you suggest to a believer who has never been to war?

_____

_____

Lesson 2
FoeTo Shop: Can I Put My Enemy's Humanity Back in the Picture?

There is a computer program that allows a person to change a photograph after the picture was taken. It would be nice if a similar program could be created for the images people store in their brains. For many veterans the mental image he or she has of their enemy is part of the reason they cannot heal from their time at war. In his book, *War and the Soul*, clinical psychologist Edward Tick states that de-humanizing one's enemy is the necessary first step on the journey from citizen to military killing machine.[7] History supports Dr. Tick's opinion. During just the last one hundred years, even in "Christian" America, military training turned our enemies from people into "Krauts", "nips", "dinks" and "towel-heads."[8] Dr. Tick warns that veterans are in a precarious psychological predicament if the humanity of their enemy ever returns in the years after the war.[9]

Retired VA psychiatrist Jonathan Shay disagrees with Dr. Tick. In his book, *Achilles in Vietnam*, Dr. Shay lists "honoring the enemy" as an essential part of any veteran's recovery from the trauma of war.[10] The Bible supports Dr. Shay's assessment. God's people are never allowed to ignore the humanity of their enemies. In Proverbs and in Romans, believers are instructed, "If your enemies are hungry, give them something to eat. And if they are thirsty, give them something to drink."[11] During his earthly life Jesus told his disciples "I did not come to bring peace, but a sword"[12] and yet he commanded his followers "Love your enemies and pray for those who persecute you".[13]

The challenge for returning warriors who performed their duties with a de-humanized view of his or her enemy is to restore the humanity of their enemy. This is particularly difficult for veterans who lost a close friend or who themselves killed people while deployed. Yet this is exactly the transformation God himself has to make towards us. He overlooks our status as his former enemies who were responsible for the death of his Son.[14]

OLD TESTAMENT LESSON: Jonah 4:1—11 CEV

Jonah was really upset and angry. So he prayed: Our LORD, I knew from the very beginning that you wouldn't destroy Nineveh. That's why I left my own country and headed for Spain. You are a kind and merciful God, and you are very patient. You always show love, and you don't like to punish anyone, not even foreigners. Now let me die! I'd be better off dead. The LORD replied, "What right do you have to be angry?" Jonah then left through the east gate of the city and made a shelter to protect himself from the sun. He sat under the shelter, waiting to see what would happen to Nineveh. The LORD made a vine grow up to shade Jonah's head and protect him from the sun. Jonah was very happy to have the vine, but early the next morning the LORD sent a worm to chew on the vine, and the vine dried up. During the day the LORD sent a scorching wind, and the sun beat down on Jonah's head, making him feel faint. Jonah was ready to die, and he shouted, "I wish I were dead!" But the LORD asked, "Jonah, do you have the right to be angry about the vine?" "Yes, I do," he answered, "and I'm angry enough to die." But the LORD said: You are concerned about a vine that you did not plant or take care of, a vine that grew up in one night and died the next. In that city of Nineveh there are more than a hundred twenty thousand people who cannot tell right from wrong, and many cattle are also there. Don't you think I should be concerned about that big city?

Key Concept: A believer must remember to see the enemy as part of God's "bigger picture."

COMMENTARY

Jonah was so set on the destruction of his nation's enemies that he defied God. Instead of warning the Ninevites of God's anger, he headed in the opposite direction. Only after God caught Jonah's attention by having a giant fish swallow the prophet does Jonah carry out his instructions. Chapter Four makes it clear that Jonah has not had a change of heart towards the Ninevites. God chastises Jonah for caring more about an environmental issue than the humanity of the Ninevites slated for destruction. Applying the lesson of the vine God had for Jonah, the 21st Century Church must realize the struggle between nations for land and supremacy, with the concomitant taking of human life, does not ever erase the fact that our enemies are also made in the image of God.

QUESTIONS FOR REFLECTION

In the New Testament Jesus taught that the Ninevites of Jonah's day would judge the people of 1st century Israel (Mt 12:41). Do you think that the people listening to Jesus still did not accept the humanity of their ancient foes?

_____

_____

Jonah comes to the point where he decides "it's either him or me." Reaching this decision point is a goal of modern military training. Was this "choice" used in the training that prepared you for deployment?

_____

_____

What effect does this type of thinking have on warriors? Does using your weapon to insure your own survival mandate that you consider your enemy less human than you?

_____

_____

How were you taught to view the enemy you might face in battle? Did your perception change once you were actually deployed?

_____

_____

In Abraham Lincoln's Second Inaugural Address he asked the Union forces to finish fighting the Civil War with "malice towards none." Have you ever received a similar request from one of your leaders? Is it possible to feel no malice towards your enemy and still do your duty?

_____

_____

_____

What can a person do to change how he or she thinks about their enemy? What effect does praying for your enemy have on your thought life? Does this practice change your military effectiveness?

_____

_____

_____

NEW TESTAMENT LESSON: Eph 6: 12-15 GNB

> For we are not fighting against human beings but against the wicked spiritual forces in the heavenly world, the rulers, authorities, and cosmic powers of this dark age. So put on God's armor now! Then when the evil day comes, you will be able to resist the enemy's attacks; and after fighting to the end, you will still hold your ground. So stand ready, with truth as a belt tight around your waist, with righteousness as your breastplate, and as your shoes the readiness to announce the Good News of peace.

Key Concept: The threat to our nation is not caused by enemy soldiers. It originates in the spirit that animates these warriors.

COMMENTARY

This passage builds on Lesson 1 in this study. Revelation 12 revealed that the devil has been cast out of heaven and now makes war against the followers of Jesus. According to this passage in Ephesians, human warriors are just agents of rival powers in the unseen realm. In the same way U.S. Forces do not hold enemy combatants liable for the crimes committed by their leaders, the Church is asked to realize that the people who oppose God's love are like soldiers in a foreign army. It is wrong to hate enemy combatants for following the orders of their master. When the spirit that animates their opposition to God's Kingdom is defeated they remain fellow members of the human family.

QUESTIONS FOR REFLECTION

Is it harder to remain faithful to core beliefs during a physical struggle or a spiritual struggle?

_____

_____

Some U.S. allies belong to other religions. Where do they fit in this instruction to the Church?

_____

_____

Has the use of armor while on deployment helped you better understand the Scriptures that talk about spiritual armor?

_____

_____

Does making "truth" your "belt" assist you to stand your ground in physical combat or is this equipment only helpful in spiritual warfare?

_____

_____

Have you learned any new information about your enemy since your deployment? Would this information have made it difficult to complete your war-time mission? Is it possible to inflict injuries on other people if you truly know them?

_____

_____

What other problems might be created as you find out more information on your opponent?

_____

_____

What does Jesus' curse on Judas (Mt 26:24) tell Christians about enemies who threaten their personal safety?

_____

_____

Lesson 3
Night Fighter: Does God Care How I Sleep?

When the therapeutic community created the diagnosis of "post-traumatic stress" in the 1980's, one of the markers for this psychological injury was disruption to a person's sleep cycle as a result of exposure to a deadly situation. Clinical studies support what every war veteran knows instinctively: A person never sleeps quite the same after being exposed to "the valley of the shadow of death." The Bible contains many narratives that reflect this shift in sleep habits. The inclusion of these sleep-narratives makes clear that sleep issues are spiritual issues. In the following text, Job wrestles with his faith because of his inability to experience restful sleep. Remember that Job's sleep issues grew from a seed that was sown in war.

OLD TESTAMENT LESSON: Job 7:4-16 BBE

> When I go to my bed, I say, When will it be time to get up? but the night is long, and I am turning from side to side till morning light. My flesh is covered with worms and dust; my skin gets hard and then is cracked again. My days go quicker than the cloth-worker's thread, and come to an end without hope. O, keep in mind that my life is wind: my eye will never again see good. The eye of him who sees me will see me no longer: your eyes will be looking for me, but I will be gone. A cloud comes to an end and is gone; so he who goes down into the underworld comes not up again. He will not come back to his house, and his place will have no more knowledge of him. So I will not keep my mouth shut; I will let the words come from it in the pain of my spirit, my soul will make a bitter outcry. Am I a sea, or a sea-beast, that you put a watch over me? When I say, In my bed I will have comfort, there I will get rest from my disease; Then you send dreams to me, and visions of fear; So that a hard death seems better to my soul than my pains. I have no desire for life.

Key Concept: For Job and many modern veterans the war continues every night when they shut their eyes.

COMMENTARY

Job displays a potent cocktail of symptoms that point to a traumatic stress injury. The author's injury is made worse by the fact that even his bed provides no sanctuary. The healing that usually occurs naturally during the night hours has stopped. When dawn arrives this veteran is actually more tired than when he lay down to sleep. The failure to achieve restful sleep complicates the relationship this believer has with God.

QUESTIONS FOR REFLECTION

How important is sleep in our relationship with God?

_____

_____

Is the condition of our sleep any measure of our faith? How does sleep affect our relationships with other people?

_____

_____

Job accused God as the source of his nightmares. Do modern veterans with PTSI think God is the source of their sleep issues?

_____

_____

Are "sleep" and "rest" and "sabbath" different words for the same thing? What does each represent in the spiritual part of a human being?

_____

_____

Does the military value sleep? How about American culture? Does the Church?

_____

_____

Why does God use sleep or the lack of sleep as a spiritual indicator of unresolved issues?

_____

_____

Is the ability to sleep a sign that a warrior is fully back from deployment? Are there counterfeits to restorative sleep?

_____

_____

NEW TESTAMENT LESSON: Lk 22:38-51 ESV

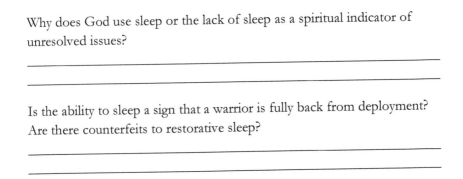

> And they said, "Look, Lord, here are two swords." And he said to them, "It is enough." And he came out and went, as was his custom, to the Mount of Olives, and the disciples followed him. And when he came to the place, he said to them, "Pray that you may not enter into temptation." And he withdrew from them about a stone's throw, and knelt down and prayed, saying, "Father, if you are willing, remove this cup from me. Nevertheless, not my will, but yours, be done." And there appeared to him an angel from heaven, strengthening him. And being in an agony he prayed more earnestly; and his sweat became like great drops of blood falling down to the ground. And when he rose from prayer, he came to the disciples and found them sleeping for sorrow, and he said to them, "Why are you sleeping? Rise and pray that you may not enter into temptation." While he was still speaking, there came a crowd, and the man called Judas, one of the twelve, was leading them. He drew near to Jesus to kiss him, but Jesus said to him, "Judas, would you betray the Son of Man with a kiss?" And when those who were around him saw what would follow, they said, "Lord, shall we strike with the sword?" And one of them struck the servant of the high priest and cut off his right ear. But Jesus said, "No more of this!" And he touched his ear and healed him.

Key Concept: The emotional state of the disciples caused them to sleep at an inappropriate time and their sleep issues caused one of them to strike out at the wrong person.

COMMENTARY

There were twelve men in the Garden of Gethsemane on the night described by this Scripture. Eleven of these individuals used sleep to cope with the stress of recent events despite their leader's need for support. The disciples' "self-medication" through sleep made them unable to discern their duty to God in a crisis situation. One of the disciples attacked a bystander while the real culprit (Judas) was untouched. Modern warriors face the same temptation to self-medicate through sleep. Clinicians note that too much sleep can be a sign of depression. Personal and professional relationships also suffer when sleep becomes a form of self-therapy. As with all gifts from God, sleep has its season.

QUESTIONS FOR REFLECTION

Reflecting on your responses in the previous Old Testament section on sleep, would you change any of your answers about the spiritual nature of sleep after this reading in the New Testament?

_____

_____

Have you ever found yourself sleeping when you wanted to be praying? Did you make any changes in order to continue praying or did sleep conquer prayer?

_____

_____

Did the disciples fail in their duty to Jesus? How serious was their lapse? How does what they did compare with falling asleep while on guard duty?

_____

_____

Was their physical/emotional weakness a sin? Do you think they needed to ask for forgiveness?

_____

_____

Should members of a unit forgive someone who falls asleep on guard duty while in a war zone? What if it caused someone else to be injured?

_____

_____

Matthew 26 contains this same incident in the Garden of Gethsemane. At verse 41 Jesus tells his disciples, "The spirit is willing, but the flesh is weak." Does this mean that the physical condition of a believer impacts their prayers more than their spiritual condition? If not, what lesson was Jesus teaching them?

_____

_____

_____

Lesson 4
Road Warrior: Does God Care How I Drive?

Unless a person participated in the wars that followed the attack on the Twin Towers, he or she probably is unaware how much war-fighting in Iraq and Afghanistan involved driving. To the uninitiated a supply convoy is not an offensive weapon that helps destroy the enemy. The simple movement of food, re-enforcements and fuel seems to lack any element of the heroic. Yet our enemies know how essential vehicular movement is to the U.S. war machine, so roads are the most common battlefield in the War on Terror. As a result, warriors drive to survive while on deployment. These habits are hard to break when a veteran comes home.

America is not the first nation to use wheeled vehicles to wage war in the Middle East. Instead of the MRAP (Mine-Resistant Ambush Protected) vehicles favored by modern forces, the ancient world used the chariot to project dominance on the battlefield. In the Bible the number and type of chariots a nation possessed was a measure of its military strength. God's people also kept track of how many drivers were available.[15]

As the following Scripture will show, driving can be an indicator of a person's spiritual condition. Even when invited to enjoy some peace, a veteran may still drive like he or she is at war.

OLD TESTAMENT LESSON: 2Ki 9:16-20 AT

> Jehu got in his chariot and went to Jezreel because his target, King Joram, was there. At the time, King Ahaziah of Judah was making a state visit to King Joram. From a guard-tower in Jezreel a sentry saw Jehu's convoy and reported it to Joram. The king instructed the sentry to send a messenger to find out if these vehicles were on a peaceful mission. So a rider went out to meet Jehu and said, "The king says, 'Peace'." And Jehu replied, "How can you offer peace? Get in my convoy!" The sentry reported to the king, "The messenger reached the vehicles but he joined their convoy instead of coming back." A second messenger was sent. When he reached the lead vehicle he announced, "The king says, 'Peace'." Jehu

replied, "How can you offer peace? Get in my convoy!" Again the sentry had to report to the king, "The messenger reached the vehicles but he joined their convoy instead of coming back. The lead vehicle looks like it is being operated by Jehu ben-Nimshi because he drives like he has road-rage."

Key Concept: The residue of war can be present in a veteran's driving even when he is serving God in another capacity.

COMMENTARY

The chariot Jehu drove was not a leisure vehicle. It was an instrument of war capable of killing people with its speed and bulk. Jehu was comfortable with his own driving habits but the intensity of his driving made other people nervous. Even when he was just going from point A to point B, Jehu drove like he was under fire. His chariot was a reflection of his spirit.

Although not listed in the clinical standard for PTSI, there is frequent mention of veterans' deployment-related driving habits in the literature produced by those who work with returning warriors.[16] Therapists acknowledge that veterans who drive offensively are responding to an inner compulsion. Christians may recognize "inner compulsions" as a euphemism for an unmet spiritual need. For this reason the local church and the veterans who are part of the congregation should address any deployment related driving issues from a spiritual perspective.

QUESTIONS FOR REFLECTION

Is the behavior of the two messengers in this narrative a common response to bad drivers? Do most people just fall in and keep their mouth shut?

_____

_____

What issues related to driving are common in the Church? Is there a difference between an impaired senior citizen who cannot safely operate a vehicle and a veteran with deployment driving habits?

_____

_____

Does your church have any ministries that center around vehicle operations? Are the drivers seen as "ministers" or just "transporters"? Does the sanctuary of the church extend to these vehicles?

_____

_____

Do you believe that the driving habits of a person reveal anything about his or her spiritual state? What do these habits tell you?

_____

_____

Does the importance of Jehu's mission justify the way he drove his chariot? How does this relate to people today? Have you ever known anyone who excused erratic driving because he or she had something important to do?

_____

_____

How should fellow Christians approach someone who still drives like he or she is deployed? How far does your responsibility extend if this person does not receive your advice?

_____

_____

NEW TESTAMENT LESSON: Act 8:26-35 CEV

> The Lord's angel said to Philip, "Go south along the desert road that leads from Jerusalem to Gaza." So Philip left. An important Ethiopian official happened to be going along that road in his chariot. He was the chief treasurer for Candace, the Queen of Ethiopia. The official had gone to Jerusalem to worship and was now on his way home. He was sitting in his chariot, reading the book of the prophet Isaiah. The Spirit told Philip to catch up with

the chariot. Philip ran up close and heard the man reading aloud from the book of Isaiah. Philip asked him, "Do you understand what you are reading?" The official answered, "How can I understand unless someone helps me?" He then invited Philip to come up and sit beside him. The man was reading the passage that said, "He was led like a sheep on its way to be killed. He was silent as a lamb whose wool is being cut off, and he did not say a word. He was treated like a nobody and did not receive a fair trial. How can he have children, if his life is snatched away?" The official said to Philip, "Tell me, was the prophet talking about himself or about someone else?" So Philip began at this place in the Scriptures and explained the good news about Jesus.

Key Concept: God can use even the time spent in government vehicles (or any vehicle) to his purpose.

COMMENTARY

Here are the highlights of this Scripture: The Treasury Secretary for Ethiopia was multi-tasking while traveling in his government vehicle. Although his body was driving, his spirit was far away. Competent as he was in his secular profession, the official was struggling to understand the truth claims of the Bible after his time at "church" (the Temple). Into the even smaller "church" of this man's vehicle, God interposed a minister who could address the official's spiritual needs.

QUESTIONS FOR REFLECTION

Was it wrong (not holy) for the official to multi-task? Does God require our full attention when we are doing spiritual work?

_____

_____

If the official had been traveling on "government time" what issues might this incident raise today?

_____

_____

Why do you think God decided to have Philip meet this official in his vehicle rather than connecting with the official when he was at the Temple?

_____

_____

Would the presence of other passengers have changed the experience for the official? How about for Philip? Have you ever been in a vehicle where other passengers controlled the spiritual environment for all the occupants?

_____

_____

Are all passengers "safe" to have in your car? Are you at risk if you are exposed to unorthodox teaching while riding/driving in a car or a carpool?

_____

_____

How many hours a week do you spend driving or riding as a passenger in some vehicle? How many hours a week do you spend in church or prayer? What is the correct balance of time spent between these two activities?

_____

_____

What spiritual resources are available for travelers? What is the relationship between the teachings a person receives through various outside media and the teachings this person receives from his or her pastor?

_____

_____

Lesson 5

Divine Failure: Can I be Disappointed with God?

Psalm 91 was the most widely distributed Scripture of Operation Iraqi Freedom (OIF) and Operation Enduring Freedom (OEF). The text of this ancient hymn was silkscreened onto bandanas and inscribed onto dog-tags by Christian organizations and sent to the warriors fighting the War on Terror. Particularly popular were verses 5-7 that promise "You need not fear any dangers at night or sudden attacks during the day or the plagues that strike in the dark or the evils that kill in daylight. A thousand may fall dead beside you, ten thousand all around you, but you will not be harmed."[17] Everyone who recited this psalm before facing an enemy threat hoped to be the recipient of this divine promise. But the simple truth remains that some of our people who were killed by enemy fire were wearing Psalm 91 bandanas or dog-tags at the moment of their death.

A Scripture passage that did not appear on any Christian souvenirs was Psalm 44. In this text a group of warriors in Ancient Israel complain that faithfulness to God did not prevent bad things from happening to them. The possibility of divine inertia is not an easy message for chaplains and pastors to share with the troops. But many veterans cite the absence of full disclosure by the church as the reason that their experience of war was even more traumatic than it needed to be. These veterans expected their faith to act as body-armor to protect them from the worst parts of war, but instead, they were subjected to physical and spiritual mutilation just like any other mortal.

It may be that you or someone at your church is a traumatized veteran who has similar grievances against God based on their experiences. He or she may have grown up listening to stories of divine protection of military units in a previous war. Or this person may have been given assurances from a well-intentioned believer that no harm ever befalls the righteous. The next section of this book is intended to draw out each veteran's expectation of the covenant God has with those he gifts for war.

OLD TESTAMENT LESSON: Ps 44 GNB

With our own ears we have heard it, O God--- our ancestors have told us about it, about the great things you did in their time, in the days of long ago: how you yourself drove out the heathen and established your people in their land; how you punished the other nations and caused your own to prosper. Your people did not conquer the land with their swords; they did not win it by their own power; it was by your power and your strength, by the assurance of your presence, which showed that you loved them. You are my king and my God; you give victory to your people, and by your power we defeat our enemies. I do not trust in my bow or in my sword to save me; but you have saved us from our enemies and defeated those who hate us. We will always praise you and give thanks to you forever.

But now you have rejected us and let us be defeated; you no longer march out with our armies. You made us run from our enemies, and they took for themselves what was ours. You allowed us to be slaughtered like sheep; you scattered us in foreign countries. You sold your own people for a small price as though they had little value. Our neighbors see what you did to us, and they mock us and laugh at us. You have made us a joke among the nations; they shake their heads at us in scorn. I am always in disgrace; I am covered with shame from hearing the sneers and insults of my enemies and those who hate me.

All this has happened to us, even though we have not forgotten you or broken the covenant you made with us. We have not been disloyal to you; we have not disobeyed your commands. Yet you left us helpless among wild animals; you abandoned us in deepest darkness. If we had stopped worshiping our God and prayed to a foreign god, you would surely have discovered it, because you know our secret thoughts.

But it is on your account that we are being killed all the time, that we are treated like sheep to be slaughtered. Wake up, Lord! Why are you asleep? Rouse yourself! Don't reject us forever! Why are you hiding from us? Don't forget our suffering and trouble! We fall crushed to the ground; we lie defeated in the dust. Come to our aid! Because of your constant love save us!

Key Concept: These believers were shocked that their faith did not guarantee total protection and victory.

COMMENTARY

Psalm 44 shows that Americans are not the first people to expect life to be fair. These veterans of Ancient Israel were bitter because God showed preferential treatment to warriors in previous conflicts, but treated these latest veterans as second-class citizens. This inequality increased the pain of their psychological injuries.

In his book, *Achilles in Vietnam*, Dr. Jonathan Shay notes that betrayal of "what's right" is the trigger event for post-traumatic stress injury.[18] The veterans of Psalm 44 definitely believe "what's right" has been betrayed and they show many other anecdotal indicators of posttraumatic spiritual injury.

QUESTIONS FOR REFLECTION

Do you think the veterans in Psalm 44 had an accurate view of previous wars? Do today's veterans think that previous wars were better or worse than OIF and OEF?

_____

_____

Why does their enemy's opinion of God's actions add insult to injury for the veterans of Psalm 44? Do enemy celebrations broadcast on news reports effect the morale of modern veterans?

_____

_____

Does God control every event on the battlefield and in the rear areas of a warzone?

_____

_____

Does God give extra protection to warriors who are faithful? Does a person's war-time protection (or lack of protection) reflect his or her spiritual status?

_____

_____

Have you ever known a believer who felt that God had shown partiality to someone else?

_____

_____

What can you say to a person who believes God should have prevented an event from happening? Can a believer say anything on God's behalf?

_____

_____

NEW TESTAMENT LESSON: Heb 11:30-38 GW

Faith caused the walls of Jericho to fall after the Israelites marched around them for seven days. Faith led the prostitute Rahab to welcome the spies as friends. She was not killed with those who refused to obey God. What more should I say? I don't have enough time to tell you about Gideon, Barak, Samson, Jephthah, David, Samuel, and the prophets. Through faith they conquered kingdoms, did what God approved, and received what God had promised. They shut the mouths of lions, put out raging fires, and escaped death. They found strength when they were weak. They were powerful in battle and defeated other armies. Women received their loved ones back from the dead. Other believers were brutally tortured but refused to be released so that they might gain eternal life. Some were made fun of and whipped, and some were chained and put in prison. Some were stoned to death, sawed in half, and killed with swords. Some wore the skins of sheep and goats. Some were poor, abused, and mistreated. The world didn't deserve these good people.

Key Concept: The faith of certain warriors was demonstrated through military victory while other warriors demonstrated their faith by enduring physical and psychological torture.

COMMENTARY

The eleventh chapter of Hebrews gives a comprehensive picture of what warriors and their families may have to endure as part of their faith. Greatest emphasis is placed on military victory but captivity and torture are a possibility.

Christian veterans and those who minister to them should note which patriarchs are on the list of approved warriors in Hebrews 11. While some of these people were paragons of virtue, others struggled with character deficiencies. The psychological imperfections of Gideon, Samson and Jephthah add a deeper dimension to our normal expectation of "what God approve[s]". Their inclusion among the heroes of the faith is based on trust in God rather than the ability to live by the Ten Commandments. Out of this trust came their actions on the battlefield.

QUESTIONS FOR REFLECTION

According to Hebrews 11 what is God's role in faith? Does it appear the individual has to take the initiative with regards to his or her faith?

_____

_____

Was God faithful to you during your deployment? How was his faithfulness (or lack of it) shown to you?

_____

_____

How does a warrior exercise faith to "shut the mouth of lions" or "put out raging fires"? What is the modern equivalent of these drastic actions?

_____

_____

The veterans in Psalm 44 equated defeat and humiliation with spiritual infidelity. The author of Hebrews 11 commends veterans who experienced both circumstances and says they "pleased God because of their faith."[19] In your experience do modern people tend to agree with the veterans of Psalm 44 or the author of Hebrews 11?

_____

_____

Does the church prepare believers for torture and humiliation as part of their faith? How can a local church equip military members to handle this possibility?

_____

_____

If someone is broken by his or her war experience, does this indicate a lack of faith? If a veteran loses his or her faith because of their deployment, how do you think this person will react to verses 35-39?

_____

_____

Lesson 6
Invalidated: Am I a Real Warrior?

At least one in five veterans of OIF and OEF is expected to show symptoms of Posttraumatic Stress Injury.[20] Many clinicians cite "moral injury" as the source of this deployment wound. "Moral injury" means the veteran was exposed to, or participated in, an act that violated their inner compass.[21] Popular culture uses a variant of "moral injury" and assumes that PTSI is caused by exposure to combat and carnage. The majority of pastors, lay church members, and returning veterans themselves are included among those who believe that only extreme events cause PTSI.

The unfortunate corollary to PTSI extreme-event theory is that many stress-injured veterans with non-tactical jobs do not believe that the wound to their spirit is PTSI. These veterans have internalized the lack of violence in their military service to mean "I am not a real warrior." According to their understanding, the distance between themselves and any "real action" was so great they simply were never exposed to anything that would have caused their symptoms. Even some veterans who were assigned to tactical units feel they cannot really have PTSI because they never used their weapon or had weapons used against them. In agreement with popular culture, they conclude the wound to their soul must be a figment of their imagination.

The belief that only "real" warriors get Posttraumatic Stress Injury is the big lie associated with death-shadow (the spiritual name for Posttraumatic Stress Injury). Death-shadow is an equal opportunity injury. It is very democratic. Death-shadow affects anyone in a war-zone, not just SEALS and front-line warriors. Take for example Job whose life provides the most extensive examination of death-shadow in the Bible. Job was a civilian who never saw direct combat or witnessed an extreme event, yet he was undone by death-shadow through the casualty reports he received.

In this study you are asked to consider your own criteria for real warriors. Read the account that follows and place yourself among King David's troops. Which side of their discussion would you have been on?

OLD TESTAMENT LESSON: 1Sam 30:21-25 ESV

Then David came to the two hundred men who had been too exhausted to follow David, and who had been left at the brook Besor. And they went out to meet David and to meet the people who were with him. And when David came near to the people he greeted them. Then all the wicked and worthless fellows among the men who had gone with David said, "Because they did not go with us, we will not give them any of the spoil that we have recovered, except that each man may lead away his wife and children, and depart." But David said, "You shall not do so, my brothers, with what the LORD has given us. He has preserved us and given into our hand the band that came against us. WHO WOULD LISTEN TO YOU IN THIS MATTER? (v.24 emphasis added) For as his share is who goes down into the battle, so shall his share be who stays by the baggage. They shall share alike." And he made it a statute and a rule for Israel from that day forward to this day.

Key Concept: In God's eyes all veterans who participate in a deployment are equal regardless of their duties. There should be no hierarchy among Christian warriors based on operational accomplishments.

COMMENTARY

It is significant that the Bible describes a group of physically fit combat veterans as "wicked and worthless." These veterans are condemned for thinking that as military elites they were entitled to war-trophies but ordinary service members were entitled only to the necessities of life. Imagine if God applied the label "wicked and worthless" to modern veterans who think their branch of service contains the only real warriors in the U.S. military.

As a person with a heart like God's, David instituted his policy recognizing that no one ever wages war without assistance from others. Thus the question David posed in verse 24 must also be answered by the local church: Who will we listen to? Will it be only those who took part in extreme events or will we validate "those who stay with the baggage?" Unless Christians reflect God's opinion on who is a "real warrior", thousands of ordinary veterans will suffer in silence.

QUESTIONS FOR REFLECTION

What are the blessings (spoils) of war? Are there any spiritual spoils to war?

_____

_____

Are military medals the modern equivalent of spoils? Which group usually gets more medals: front-line troops or "those who stay with the baggage?"

_____

_____

Is the Purple Heart Medal (for wounds received from enemy fire) awarded to veterans with PTSI? Is this in keeping with David's instructions?

_____

_____

Why does God make veterans from the frontline equal to those who never saw combat?

_____

_____

Does the non-military part of society operate according to the egalitarian way David commanded? How are "spoils" (financial incentives) divided in the business world?

_____

_____

Why would God have veterans model a different way than other professions?

_____

_____

Does the Church have jobs that are considered "frontline" and other types of service that are considered "baggage guards"? What types of ministry fit into each category?

_____

_____

NEW TESTAMENT LESSON: Php 2: 25-30 GW

> I feel that I must send Epaphroditus-my brother, coworker, and fellow soldier-back to you. You sent him as your personal representative to help me in my need. He has been longing to see all of you and is troubled because you heard that he was sick. Indeed, he was so sick that he almost died. But God had mercy not only on him but also on me and kept me from having one sorrow on top of another. So I'm especially eager to send him to you. In this way you will have the joy of seeing him again and I will feel relieved. Give him a joyful Christian welcome. Make sure you honor people like Epaphroditus highly. He risked his life and almost died for the work of Christ in order to make up for the help you couldn't give me.

Key Concept: Though the risks are different health care workers and other support staff are just as vital to mission accomplishment.

COMMENTARY

Epaphroditus was sent by the citizens of Phillipi to help Paul with the administrative side of Paul's foreign ministry. Epaphroditus ended up being Paul's nurse when he was incapacitated. The disease that struck down Paul nearly killed Epaphroditus. No other member of Epaphroditus' community was at risk to contract this disease because they did not venture out beyond their borders. If Epaphroditus also had chosen to stay home, he too, would have been in no danger. Despite the unexpected threat that came upon Epaphroditus, the citizens of Phillipi have to be reminded to honor soldiers, like Epaphroditus, who serve as clerks and nurses. The author of this epistle is afraid these citizens do not realize the cost everyone who deploys may have to pay for their service.

QUESTIONS FOR REFLECTION

Although Epaphroditus was not wounded in combat he still nearly became a statistic. Do you think American society believes all warriors are at risk of being wounded by their deployment?

_____

_____

Epaphroditus was more concerned for the citizens of Phillipi than he was for himself. How do modern warriors feel about the folks back home?

_____

_____

Which soldier of the Lord was more important to mission accomplishment-Paul or Epaphroditus? What determines a person's value while deployed?

_____

_____

Who is more wounded- a veteran who was hit by enemy fire or a veteran with PTSI? Is this a choice a congregation has to make?

_____

_____

Does a hierarchy of wounds or type of service among veterans strengthen the church?

_____

_____

Lesson 7
I am Legend: Will My Story Injure Me?

The previous study looked at the spiritual consequences for veterans if they do not consider their war-story is valid. This study is similar because it also relates to how a veteran interprets his or her time at war. Rather than self-imposed silence though, the topic under consideration here is how a veteran can be injured by his or her own negative self-talk.

There are physical injuries, like Carpal Tunnel Syndrome, caused by performing the same action over and over again. Repeating the same story over and over again is how legends start. "I am Legend" is the label used in this study to describe a self-inflicted injury caused by repetition of: 1) a negative self-description; 2) a negative interpretation of a defining life event; or 3) Both of the preceding categories. The wound caused by cyclic self-cursing is low self-esteem and an increase in the severity and duration of Posttraumatic Stress Injury.

Self-cursing, as part of war-related death-shadow, has two components: a stressor from deployment and the interpretation of the stressor by the individual. Any event, even an incident that occurs back in the U.S., can provide the first part of this cycle. Take for example a warrior who left behind his or her family in order to deploy. If harm comes to someone in the family while this service member is deployed, he or she may decide that protecting foreign nationals was the wrong thing to do. As this warrior begins to give voice to this interpretation of events no amount of body armor will protect his or her soul from being pierced by blame and regret.

As you read the account that follows, think about your own interpretation of the time you spent deployed. Consider whether your life has been improved or constrained by the meaning you give to the time spent at war.

OLD TESTAMENT LESSON: 2Sam 16:5-14 GNB

> When King David arrived at Bahurim, one of Saul's relatives, Shimei son of Gera, came out to meet him, cursing him as he came. Shimei started throwing stones at David and his officials, even though David was surrounded by his men and his bodyguards. Shimei cursed him and said, "Get out! Get out! Murderer! Criminal! You took Saul's kingdom, and now the LORD is punishing you for murdering so many of Saul's family. The LORD has given the kingdom to your son Absalom, and you are ruined, you murderer!" Abishai, whose mother was Zeruiah, said to the king, "Your Majesty, why do you let this dog curse you? Let me go over there and cut off his head!" "This is none of your business," the king said to Abishai and his brother Joab. "If he curses me because the LORD told him to, who has the right to ask why he does it?" And David said to Abishai and to all his officials, "My own son is trying to kill me; so why should you be surprised at this Benjaminite? The LORD told him to curse; so leave him alone and let him do it. Perhaps the LORD will notice my misery and give me some blessings to take the place of his curse." So David and his men continued along the road. Shimei kept up with them, walking on the hillside; he was cursing and throwing stones and dirt at them as he went. The king and all his men were worn out when they reached the Jordan, and there they rested.

Key Concept: David began to believe somebody else's interpretation of his deployment and it caused injury to himself and those he loved.

COMMENTARY

David knew that God had removed Saul as king and placed David on the throne of Israel. So it is surprising to find David passive in the face of Shimei's lies. Even his counselors are puzzled by David's acceptance of these verbal jabs. The explanation for David's lethargy is found in his interpretation of events. For David, Shimei's persecution is just an extension of God's judgment on David's earlier adultery. This interpretation does not correspond with what God actually said (2Sam 12:10-11). While

78

David's son (Absalom) had fulfilled some of God's verdict on the king's affair, none of Shimei's maledictions were part of God's sanctions. Nor did God promise David that bearing up under this (or any) persecution would restore David's life to what he had known in better days. The suffering of David and his entourage was unnecessary and was the direct result of David's own negative interpretation of events.

QUESTIONS FOR REFLECTION

Do you think Shimei's taunt was the first time David heard Saul's relatives accuse him of being a murderer? Are warriors sometimes called "murderer" today? If these charges were repeated among David's cabinet members, could this have affected David's interpretation of events?

_____

_____

Do families play a part in helping a veteran find meaning (or lack of meaning) in his or her military service? Does the military recognize the influence of family on a warrior's career decisions?

_____

_____

Both David and Shimei believed David's situation was the result of God's wrath. Do most people blame divine displeasure when life is not proceeding as expected? How can a veteran determine the truth of such a claim? How can a veteran's friends counter such an interpretation if it is baseless?

_____

_____

The members of David's unit also suffered because of their leader's interpretation of events. What effect does the story a veteran tells himself/herself (or allow others to say about their service) have on the lives of his or her closest friends and family?

_____

_____

At the time David arrived in this village his military position was precarious. Does the military outcome of a war determine how a veteran interprets their service?

_____

_____

Did you ever experience personal losses while you were deployed? What was your reaction? Did you blame anyone? How do you talk about it now?

_____

_____

_____

What was God's part in your losses? Have you ever spoken your answer to this question out loud to another person?

_____

_____

NEW TESTAMENT LESSON: Jam 3:4-9 CEV

> It takes strong winds to move a large sailing ship, but the captain uses only a small rudder to make it go in any direction. Our tongues are small too, and yet they brag about big things. It takes only a spark to start a forest fire! The tongue is like a spark. It is an evil power that dirties the rest of the body and sets a person's entire life on fire with flames that come from hell itself. All kinds of animals, birds, reptiles, and sea creatures can be tamed and have been tamed. But our tongues get out of control. They are restless and evil, and always spreading deadly poison. My dear friends, with our tongues we speak both praises and curses. We praise our Lord and Father, and we curse people who were created to be like God, and this isn't right.

Key Concept: The tongue can cause more harm than a flame-thrower and its use should be treated just as cautiously.

COMMENTARY

Many factors influence the course of a believer's life. James 3 presents a strong case that the tongue plays a central role. Christians are warned that the default setting of the tongue is "negative". Great intentionality is necessary to avoid injuring self and others. Similarly the author points out a flaw common among believers: we exercise self-discipline in so many aspects of our life and yet let the tongue go AWOL.

QUESTIONS FOR REFLECTION

How does this warning about the power of the spoken word line up with our Constitution's protection of free speech? Are there any secular limits on the words we say?

_____

_____

What American icons model the negative behavior the New Testament is describing? On the other hand, can you name a public figure known for restraining his or her tongue?

_____

_____

The old proverb, "If you can't say something nice about somebody don't say anything at all" is left over from a time when our culture took the instructions in James 3 seriously. Are there modern sayings that contain the same message of restraining our speech?

_____

_____

How do you describe yourself? Do you treat yourself the same way you treat others with what you say?

_____

_____

How do you describe your deployment? Do you ever denigrate your service because you do not believe your sacrifice was as large as other military members?

_____

_____

Does the church have a role to play in helping veterans to tell their self-narratives safely? What is that role? Does "safely" mean that all stories have to be happy?

_____

_____

Lesson 8
Inner Vows: Was I Talking To God or the devil?

In the Old Testament a vow was considered a religious act. Priests at the Temple were given precise instructions for handling vows separately from other acts of worship.[22] God did not require his followers to make vows as part of their religious practice, but if a person did make a vow, it was a sin not to perform the sacrifice that was promised.[23]

The New Testament changed the focal point of worship from the Temple in Jerusalem to the temple that exists in each believer. This transition made the Christian community a kingdom of priests, just as God promised.[24] Yet not many of today's priests of the inner temple seem to know that vows are still a sacred act. As a consequence Christians make vows on a daily basis. Some are made publicly, but many more are made in their souls. For example, when someone tells himself or herself that he or she will never forgive a certain person, that man or woman is making an inner vow. Another popular inner vow is to swear never to participate in activities where shame and embarrassment are a possibility. The most common inner vows made by deployed military personnel begin like this, "If I ever get out of here alive I will never . .." These self-promises often concern survival, behavior under fire, and forgiveness towards self, fellow warriors and/or the enemy.

The holy and binding nature of a vow has not changed regardless of which Testament covers its maker. If anything, inner vows are even more powerful than their ancient public precursor because of their hidden and soul-level origins. Like a secret app hidden in a computer's programming, an inner vow can tie a believer to a moment in his or her life. Years after the event this same person may wonder why his or her life has withered rather than grown. In the case of a veteran, being tied to a deployment inner vow means never being able to leave their war truly in the past.

OLD TESTAMENT LESSON: Jdg 11: 28-36, 39 GW

But the king of Ammon didn't listen to the message Jephthah sent him. Then the LORD'S Spirit came over Jephthah. Jephthah went through Gilead, Manasseh, and Mizpah in Gilead to gather an army. From Mizpah in Gilead Jephthah went to attack Ammon. Jephthah made a vow to the LORD. He said, "If you will really hand Ammon over to me, then whatever comes out of the doors of my house to meet me when I return safely from Ammon will belong to the LORD. I will sacrifice it as a burnt offering." So Jephthah went to fight against Ammon. The LORD handed the people of Ammon over to him.. . It was a decisive defeat. So the Ammonites were crushed by the people of Israel. When Jephthah went to his home in Mizpah, he saw his daughter coming out to meet him. She was dancing with tambourines in her hands. She was his only child. Jephthah had no other sons or daughters. When he saw her, he tore his clothes in grief and said, "Oh no, Daughter! You've brought me to my knees! What disaster you've brought me! I made a foolish promise to the LORD. Now I can't break it." She said to him, "Father, you made a promise to the LORD. Do to me whatever you promised since the LORD has punished your enemy Ammon.". . . He did to her what he had vowed, and she never had a husband.

Key Concept: When a person makes a vow he or she is engaging in high risk behavior.

COMMENTARY

Jephthah already had God's favor. He did not need to entice God to bless him through an inner vow. Judging by Jephthah's reaction to his daughter's greeting it is obvious that he never intended for his vow to encompass the sacrifice of his child. Unintended consequences are an intrinsic component of inner vows. This is the reason that God warns us so strongly to avoid such behavior. Every person is born already in debt to God for his or her life. God never asks for repayment of that debt. Making a vow to do some act or make a particular sacrifice not only increases our indebtedness to God, it creates an obligation that is not covered by Jesus' sacrifice on the cross. In the case of Jephthah, and many modern veterans, the cost of inner-vows made during deployment fall heaviest on innocent family members.

QUESTIONS FOR REFLECTION

Since God warns us in the Bible about the high cost of making a religious vow[25], why do you think people still make spiritual vows?

_____

_____

Is there any positive result that comes from making a vow?

_____

_____

Why would God have such strong feelings toward unfulfilled vows as compared to other human shortcomings?

_____

_____

How would you describe the effects of being in debt to God?

_____

_____

Does the military ask its members to make vows? Does the church? When or why?

_____

_____

Do you think people with no knowledge of Scripture still feel guilty if they break their promises to God?

_____

_____

Is there any secular or spiritual way to compensate for an unfulfilled vow?

_____

_____

NEW TESTAMENT LESSON: Mt 5:33-37 GNB

"You have also heard that people were told in the past, 'Do not break your promise, but do what you have vowed to the Lord to do.' But now I tell you: do not use any vow when you make a promise. Do not swear by heaven, for it is God's throne; nor by earth, for it is the resting place for his feet; nor by Jerusalem, for it is the city of the great King. Do not even swear by your head, because you cannot make a single hair white or black. Just say 'Yes' or 'No'---anything else you say comes from the Evil One.. ."

Key Concept: It is not God who prompts a believer to anchor a promise with a vow.

COMMENTARY

God is the only person who can say, "I swear to God" without committing a sin.[26] Ever since the Garden of Eden people have been deceived into to thinking they could be like God and this extends to making inner-vows. The Bible reveals that even when a person thinks he or she is the only party to the vow, the spiritual reality is every creature needs a higher power to consent to their oath.[27] This narrows a person's possible choices for consent down to one of two possibilities: God or the devil.

Jesus had a simple rule he taught his disciples for making an acceptable vow to God: "Don't." He explained that a vow is dependent on future conditions beyond the resources of the speaker. This is why making a vow (or swearing an oath) is a sin. Such a declaration steals power from an object the speaker has no legal right to use. As Jesus reminds his disciples in this paragraph, we do not even have authority to use our own bodies as collateral.

QUESTIONS FOR REFLECTION

What sort of things do modern people swear by when they try to convince other people that they are sincere?

_____

_____

Why does the New Testament change the status of vows? Is it related to Jesus' sacrifice on the cross?

_____

_____

Have you ever made an inner vow where you promised yourself not to repeat a particular activity ever again? What was it?

_____

_____

Is it part of human nature to make such vows? Does God make vows?

_____

_____

Do you think unfulfilled vows keep people from coming to church and/or being able to re-enter society after a deployment?

_____

_____

Who can release a veteran from a vow he or she made while under fire or during some other type of crisis?

_____

_____

Lesson 9
Wrong Dog-Tags: What if the Church Thinks I am Somebody Else?

It is uncomfortable for anyone to enter a new community. Going to church for the first time, or returning to church after an absence, is like entering a new community. The most common way of dealing with this discomfort is to camouflage one's true personality and attempt to look, or act, like the group. This was not what Jesus had in mind for the tomb-man of Gadara. Jesus sent this warrior back to his hometown to show how much he had changed since his people had last seen him.[28]

Even if a modern veteran was a member of a church before he or she went off to war, this service member will return from war a different person. Change is a natural reaction to an environment, like war, where the eternal happens. A similar transformation occurs in other life-passage events like confirmation, baptism and marriage. In each of these events the believer is changed in relationship to the church. The tendency, among those who stay behind, is to treat the individual in the same manner as his or her pre-transformational self. It takes intentionality from both the transformed person and the church to let the new identity of this person be established in a way that is authentic to what God has done in this man or woman.

OLD TESTAMENT LESSON: 1Sam 17:31-40 CEV

Some soldiers overheard David talking, so they told Saul what David had said. Saul sent for David, and David came. "Your Majesty," he said, "this Philistine shouldn't turn us into cowards. I'll go out and fight him myself!" "You don't have a chance against him," Saul replied. "You're only a boy, and he's been a soldier all his life." But David told him: Your Majesty, I take care of my father's sheep. And when one of them is dragged off by a lion or a bear, I go after it and beat the wild animal until it lets the sheep go. If the wild animal turns and attacks me, I grab it by the throat and kill it. Sir, I have killed lions and bears that way, and I can kill this worthless Philistine. He shouldn't have made fun of the army of the living God! The LORD has rescued me from the claws of lions and bears, and he will keep me safe from the hands of this Philistine. "All right," Saul answered, "go ahead and fight him. And I hope the LORD will help you." Saul had his own military clothes and armor put on David, and he gave David a bronze helmet to wear. David strapped on a sword and tried to walk around, but he was not used to wearing those things. "I can't move with all this stuff on," David said. "I'm just not used to it." David took off the armor and picked up his shepherd's stick. He went out to a stream and picked up five smooth rocks and put them in his leather bag. Then with his sling in his hand, he went straight toward Goliath.

Key Concept: David had to resist Saul's attempt to make him conform to Saul's idea of a warrior.

COMMENTARY

In the Scripture Saul tries to change David into a copy of himself. Saul expected David to mimic his methods of dealing with problems. David had enough life experience to recognize that Saul's ways would not work for him. David also was able to see parallels between warfare and his civilian occupation. Not everyone is able to make these connections. Therefore, when a veteran returns, the first task of the local church is to help the veteran determine his or her post-deployment identity.

QUESTIONS FOR REFLECTION

Saul wrapped himself in armor and worked up close. David needed mobility and some distance from his problems. How do you work in a challenging environment?

_____

_____

Was there any time in your military service that, like David, the chain of command did not want you to operate according to your natural abilities? How did you react? Was that a comfortable experience for you?

_____

_____

Do you think you changed during your deployment? Has anyone tried to make you go back to who you were before or become someone you have never been?

_____

_____

Do people who have never been in the military expect a veteran to behave according to certain habits? What are these expectations?

_____

_____

How are "church-people" or "Christians" supposed to act? Have you ever tried to behave in this way? When?

_____

_____

Have you ever described yourself by your job or military service? What other aspects of your life do you identify yourself by?

_____

_____

NEW TESTAMENT LESSON: 1Co 12: 4-12 CEV

> There are different kinds of spiritual gifts, but they all come from the same Spirit. There are different ways to serve the same Lord, and we can each do different things. Yet the same God works in all of us and helps us in everything we do. The Spirit has given each of us a special way of serving others. Some of us can speak with wisdom, while others can speak with knowledge, but these gifts come from the same Spirit. To others the Spirit has given great faith or the power to heal the sick or the power to work mighty

miracles. Some of us are prophets, and some of us recognize when God's Spirit is present. Others can speak different kinds of languages, and still others can tell what these languages mean. But it is the Spirit who does all this and decides which gifts to give to each of us. The body of Christ has many different parts, just as any other body does.

Key Concept: God's plan is for each church to contain people of diverse spiritual abilities.

COMMENTARY

The 12th chapter of 1 Corinthians is addressed to a congregation struggling with the problem of peer pressure. God had called together people with various spiritual abilities but there was a movement in that church to make everyone act and worship in the same way. These believers had to be reminded that the variations they were trying to suppress were actually manifestations of God.

Peer pressure still exists in the modern church. People are most comfortable when others experience God exactly as they have. Conversely God wants each of his children to love and serve their Creator according to who that person was created to be.

QUESTIONS FOR REFLECTION

Do you have any of the gifts mentioned in this Scripture? How has God worked through you in the past?

_____

_____

What gift (s) do those who have participated in war bring to the body of Christ?

_____

_____

Has God used your deployment(s) to reveal abilities you did not know you possessed? If so, can this ability be used in a peace-time setting?

_____

_____

What can a veteran receive from those in the body of Christ who have never been in the military?

_____

_____

Do all Christians need to look and act the same?

_____

_____

Why does God want his church to consist of people with divergent gifts and experiences?

_____

_____

Lesson 10
On a Pedestal: Can I Still Be Your Hero If I Am Not Perfect?

Television journalist Tom Brokaw wrote a book about the men and woman who fought in World War II called "The Greatest Generation." Brokaw lionized these veterans for their resiliency in surviving the Great Depression, defeating Axis aggression and building the economic superpower that America became after the war. The moniker "Greatest Generation" has become the culturally accepted image for the veterans of the 1940's and thus disguises the reality of isolationism, racial segregation and black-marketeering that were trademarks of U.S. society during this conflict.

An analogous misrepresentation of current veterans is gaining traction in American culture today. One indicator is the unabashed use of the title "hero" by veteran-support organizations to describe everyone who has served in Iraq and Afghanistan. When combined with spontaneous standing ovations on airplanes and public sporting events, and institutional policies that mandate expressions of gratitude to anyone who is identified as a member of the military, the stage is set for unrealistic expectations in the minds of the public and our veterans.

There is a maxim that says, "I am not who I think I am. I am not who you think I am. I am who I think you think I am."[29] This statement summarizes the spiritual issue that is the focus of this study. If a veteran is constantly called "hero" by the members of his or her church, it is extremely difficult to go against the culture of praise and admit a personal struggle with impure thoughts, or selfishness, or moral cowardice, or a thousand other peccadilloes. Rather than disappoint their adoring community, veterans find it is easier to stay silent and postpone the spiritual repair of their soul until they are a little less exalted. Unfortunately this delay (and silence) solidifies the perception of immaculate heroism and makes future contrition nearly impossible.

The Christian community and veterans themselves need to remember that everyone who joins the military today (and in generations past) came from families, communities and backgrounds that bear the imprint of the social challenges faced by their fellow citizens. Broken homes, chemical dependency and sexual abuse are just a few of the scars that already mark some service members before our nation sends them off to war. Even those who eventually are awarded the Congressional Medal of Honor for their heroism never stop being the product of their upbringing and their sin-nature.

OLD TESTAMENT LESSON: 1Sam 23: 6-14 CEV

Meanwhile, Saul heard that David was in Keilah... Saul decided to go there and surround the town, in order to trap David and his men. . . By this time, Abiathar had joined David in Keilah and had brought along everything he needed to get answers from God. David heard about Saul's plan to capture him, and he told Abiathar, "Let's ask God what we should do." David prayed, "LORD God of Israel, I was told that Saul is planning to come here. What should I do? Suppose he threatens to destroy the town because of me. Would the leaders of Keilah turn me over to Saul? Or is he really coming? Please tell me, LORD." "Yes, he will come," the LORD answered. David asked, "Would the leaders of Keilah hand me and my soldiers over to Saul?" "Yes, they would," the LORD answered. David and his six hundred men got out of there fast and started moving from place to place. . . David stayed in hideouts in the hill country of Ziph Desert. Saul kept searching, but God never let Saul catch him.

Key Concept: The greatest warrior in the Bible shared his troubles with the community of faith and was able to find the answers he needed.

COMMENTARY

By the time David was hiding in Keilah he knew what it was to be adored as a hero. There had been a time in his life when the female population of Jerusalem used to sing about his military exploits.[30] David also knew how fickle public opinion could be. When he was kicked out of Saul's government the only people who would serve with David were the dregs of society.[31]

94

Abiathar had known David when he was a star, and when David was an outlaw. Even though David was a war hero who had defeated giants, Abiathar approached David just as a man who desperately needed answers from God.

QUESTIONS FOR REFLECTION

David's problems were a mixture of military and political issues. Do you think there are many modern generals who would bring these types of problems to their pastor? How about their Sunday School class?

_____

_____

God often talked to David directly. Why do you think God made David consult Abiathar on this occasion?

_____

_____

Does military culture allow leaders to share their problems with their command? Would it effect the subordinates perception of their leader if he or she revealed his or her personal struggles? How about the perception of the congregation towards their church leaders?

_____

_____

Is it difficult for veterans to talk about deployment issues with people who have no military background?

_____

_____

Do you think veterans are affected by the congregation's perception of the military? Why might a veteran be reluctant to disappoint another person's expectations?

_____

_____

Do you think it is possible to be both a "hero" and a "sinner" in a local church? Does one preclude the other?

_____

_____

NEW TESTAMENT LESSON: 1Co 1:26-31 CEV

> My dear friends, remember what you were when God chose you. The people of this world didn't think that many of you were wise. Only a few of you were in places of power, and not many of you came from important families. But God chose the foolish things of this world to put the wise to shame. He chose the weak things of this world to put the powerful to shame. What the world thinks is worthless, useless, and nothing at all is what God has used to destroy what the world considers important. God did all this to keep anyone from bragging to him. You are God's children. He sent Christ Jesus to save us and to make us wise, acceptable, and holy. So if you want to brag, do what the Scriptures say and brag about the Lord.

Key Concept: The only hero the Church is supposed to have is Jesus. Everybody else is a work in progress.

COMMENTARY

It is clear from later parts of this letter that hero worship was rife among this faith community. This plea to the Corinthian church was intended to reset their thinking. Amnesia had set in and people had forgotten what a mess they were when they first came down to the altar. This memory lapse allowed bragging and one-upmanship to flourish. The instructions in these verses recalled the church to a counter-cultural mindset. In the context of this study, this mindset means looking past the uniform and campaign ribbons and seeing yourself or any veteran as just another person who needs to share his or her burdens with God's people.

QUESTIONS FOR REFLECTION

Why was it necessary to remind the believers in Corinth of their origins? How long do you think these people had been Christians?

_____

_____

Do people who have been Christian for a long time act differently than they did when they were new believers?

_____

_____

What is your reaction when a stranger thanks you for your service? Do you have a different reaction when the other person is also a veteran?

_____

_____

Are there veterans who thrive on being heroes? Do some veterans resist sharing events from their past if the experience was not heroic?

_____

_____

Is there an innate desire in human nature to appear wise by the standards of the world? Does this desire make it difficult for a "hero" to admit he or she is struggling in an area of their life?

_____

_____

How many years should a believer talk about their "humble origins" (who he or she was before conversion)? Do you think revealing this information would help a veteran to open up about his or her struggles?

_____

_____

Lesson 11

Conscientious Objectors: Should I Worship With People Who Reject My Profession?

When the U.S. House of Representatives approved H.R. 748: The Universal National Service Act on February 15, 2013, it contained an exemption from military service for those persons who are "conscientious objectors." The bill states in section 108:

> Nothing in this title shall be construed to require a person to be subject to combatant training and service in the uniformed services, if that person, by reason of sincerely held moral, ethical, or religious beliefs, is conscientiously opposed to participation in war in any form.

In the Bible verses that accompany this study God grants a much broader exemption from military service than do the members of Congress. Although God is the one who issues a general call for his people to wage war, he also allows for those who do not cope with the strain of war to go home. The exemptions God grants to his people illustrate that God values marriage and society over military exploits. His instructions for personnel screening make for a smaller, more cohesive force. God is not worried that too many people will leave because of their conscientious objections. God's presence allows for even a small force to defeat numerically superior enemies.

In Ancient Israel, after victory had been achieved, those who went to war returned to live among those who decided not to fight. The one occasion when the people of Israel did not tolerate conscientious objectors nearly caused the extinction of the tribe of Benjamin.[32] The important lesson for veterans in the Church to gain from these instructions is that, on the subject of war, diversity of conscience is to be part of the Christian community.

OLD TESTAMENT LESSON: Deut 20:1-9 ESV

"When you go out to war against your enemies, and see horses and chariots and an army larger than your own, you shall not be afraid of them, for the LORD your God is with you, who brought you up out of the land of Egypt. And when you draw near to the battle, the priest shall come forward and speak to the people and shall say to them, 'Hear, O Israel, today you are drawing near for battle against your enemies: let not your heart faint. Do not fear or panic or be in dread of them, for the LORD your God is he who goes with you to fight for you against your enemies, to give you the victory.' Then the officers shall speak to the people, saying, 'Is there any man who has built a new house and has not dedicated it? Let him go back to his house, lest he die in the battle and another man dedicate it. And is there any man who has planted a vineyard and has not enjoyed its fruit? Let him go back to his house, lest he die in the battle and another man enjoy its fruit. And is there any man who has betrothed a wife and has not taken her? Let him go back to his house, lest he die in the battle and another man take her.' And the officers shall speak further to the people, and say, 'Is there any man who is fearful and fainthearted? Let him go back to his house, lest he make the heart of his fellows melt like his own.' And when the officers have finished speaking to the people, then commanders shall be appointed at the head of the people.

Key Concept: Not every citizen is called to have a part in war.

COMMENTARY

This passage from Deuteronomy is counter-intuitive to American military thinking. In the U.S. military it is the officers who give the motivational speeches before battle and it is the chaplains who screen the conscientious objectors for discharge. As these verses illustrate, in Ancient Israel it was the chaplain (priest) who inspired the troops for battle and the officers who offered exemptions for qualifying service members to go back home.

At first glance the Biblical roles assigned to chaplain and officers appear topsy-turvy. Further reflection will reveal it is the modern system that goes against human nature. The chaplain should be the person who reminds warriors of the eternal consequences of battle because the spiritual arena is where the chaplain is gifted. In contrast the officer should be gifted in courage and duty. Only the courageous and dutiful can release someone else from duty and valor. If a chaplain offered this absolution it would not be received because the seeker would recognize that such a dispensation is not the chaplain's to give.

QUESTIONS FOR REFLECTION

Do you think it was awkward for those who left the army after this speech to be around the families of those who lost loved ones on the battlefield? Would it be difficult for these people to worship in the same church today?

_____

_____

Why do you think the clause "lest . . . another man" is present in three of the reasons a person could leave his deployment in Ancient Israel? What unfulfilled goals might make a warrior's death particularly tragic in the 21st century?

_____

_____

Does the U.S. military have any exclusions to military service based on family situations? Are there family situations that prevent a service member from deploying?

_____

_____

Today's "All-Volunteer" military has lessened the need for a person to declare his or her self to be a conscientious objector. What are the acceptable reasons that a person already in the military can be released from completing his or her contract?

_____

_____

Do you think the people who left Moses' army after this speech were any less patriotic than the people who stayed to fight the battle? Were these persons more religious or less religious than their compatriots? How about a person who applies for conscientious objector status in today's military?

_____

_____

NEW TESTAMENT LESSON: Lk 9:51-62 ESV

When the days drew near for him to be taken up, he set his face to go to Jerusalem. And he sent messengers ahead of him, who went and entered a village of the Samaritans, to make preparations for him. But the people did not receive him, because his face was set toward Jerusalem. And when his disciples James and John saw it, they said, "Lord, do you want us to tell fire to come down from heaven and consume them?" But he turned and rebuked them. And they went on to another village. As they were going along the road, someone said to him, "I will follow you wherever you go." And Jesus said to him, "Foxes have holes, and birds of the air have nests, but the Son of Man has nowhere to lay his head." To another he said, "Follow me." But he said, "Lord, let me first go and bury my father." And Jesus said to him, "Leave the dead to bury their own dead. But as for you, go and proclaim the kingdom of God." Yet another said, "I will follow you, Lord, but let me first say farewell to those at my home." Jesus said to him, "No one who puts his hand to the plow and looks back is fit for the kingdom of God."

Key Concept: For his final campaign Jesus wanted people who had no distractions. Those with economic and family issues were exempted from full-time ministry.

COMMENTARY

The disciples wanted to unleash war on the communities that did not support Jesus' ministry to Jerusalem. In this case Jesus was the conscientious objector. He reprimanded the disciples because brute force would not have served the purpose of God on that operation. However Jesus was on a deadly mission and he only wanted team members who were mentally committed to the objective. For the journey to Calvary Jesus gave exemptions to people who had conflicting loyalties and other social obligations.

QUESTIONS FOR REFLECTION

Which occupation requires more commitment or sacrifice: ministry or military service? How are these two vocations alike and how are they different?

_____

_____

Is everyone in the church called to full-time ministry? How about military service? What were the reasons people gave for not answering Jesus' call?

_____

_____

Why did Jesus seek to discourage some people from following him? Does this happen in the church today?

_____

_____

The Old Testament gave three categories of military exemptions: 1) Fear; 2) Business Start-ups; 3) Nuptials. The New Testament used three metaphors to filter Jesus' disciples: 1) Filial Duties; 2) Housing Concerns; 3) Business Concerns. How do these aspects of conscience fit in with military or Christian thinking about public service?

_____

_____

_____

_____

The Disciples wanted nothing to do with people who rejected their mission. Do people in church isolate themselves from other Christians who disagree with them?

_____

_____

How can a local church support veterans and those who disagree with military intervention? Does the pastor have to remain neutral on military service in order for the church to function?

_____

_____

CHAPTER 6 ENDNOTES

[1] Mk 5:19

[2] Lk 5:39

[3] Ecc 3:8

[4] 1Chr 23:5

[5] *Merriam-Webster's Collegiate Dictionary*, s.v "sanctuary"

[6] Job 1:6; Job 2:1

[7] Edward Tick, *War and the Soul: Healing Our Nations Veterans from Post-traumatic Stress Disorder*, 81

[8] Ibid. 82

[9] Ibid. 92

[10] Jonathan Shay, *Achilles in Vietnam,* 115

[11] Pr 25:21, Ro 12:20

[12] Mt 10:34

[13] Mt 5:44

[14] Rom 5:8-10

[15] 1Ki 4:26

[16] James Dao, "Back From War, Fear and Danger Fill Driver's Seat", *New York Times,* http://www.nytimes.com/2012/01/11/us/post-traumatic-stress-disorder-may-cause-erratic-driving.html?pagewanted=all&_r=0

[17] Psalm 91:5-7 GNB

[18] Jonathan Shay, *Achilles in Vietnam,* 6

[19] Heb 11: 39 CEV

[20] Terri Tanielian and Lisa H. Jaycox. eds, *The Invisible Wounds of War: Psychological and Cognitive Injuries, Their Consequences, and Services to Assist Recovery,* 3

[21] Brett T. Litz et al., "Moral Injury and Moral Repair," 697

[22] Num 6:2; Nu 29:39

[23] Ecc 5:4-6

[24] Ex 19:6

[25] Ecc 5:4-6

[26] Heb 6:13, Mt 5:34

[27] Heb 6:16

[28] Mk 5:19

[29] Various people (i.e. Goethe, Max Webber, Charles Cooley and others) are credited with this dictum.

[30] 1Sam 18:7

[31] 1Sam 22:2

[32] Jdg 21:5

7
CONCLUSION

Just like Jesus said, each day the news is full of wars and the rumors of war.[1] The Cold War is back from the grave and national boundaries that appeared so permanent when the guns fell silent after World War II are now in flux. In Asia the bottom of the sea is the impetus for the 21st century's first nautical arms race. Antarctica appears to be the only continent that is safe from the suicide attacks of Islamic extremists. All signs point to a constant stream of veterans needing the local church.

This book is not meant to encompass every issue that a veteran will face as he or she transitions into their local church. Rather it is offered as a tool to change non-Biblical practices towards warriors and to model a form of inquiry veterans can use to transition their experiences from the battlefield to the mission field or wherever Christ has placed them.

---

[1] Mt 24:6; Mk 13:7

8
BIBLIOGRAPHY

Adsit, Chris. *The Combat Trauma Healing Manual: Christ-centered Solutions for Combat Trauma.* Newport News, VA: Military Ministry Press, 2008.

------, Rahnella Adsit, and Marshele Carter Waddell. *When War Comes Home: Christ-Centered Healing for Wives of Combat Veterans.* Newport News, Virginia: Military Ministry Press, 2008.

Allman, Mark J. *Who Would Jesus Kill: War, Peace and the Christian Tradition.* Winona, Minnesota: Anselm Academic, 2008.

American Psychiatric Association. *Diagnostic and Statistical Manual of Mental Disorders, 4th ed., text rev.* Washington, D.C. : American Psychiatric Association, 2000.

Bainton, Roland H. *Christian Attitudes Toward War and Peace.* Nashville: Abbingdon Press, 1960.

Bosworth, David. "'You have Shed Much Blood, and Waged Great Wars': Killing, Bloodguilt, and Combat Stress." *Journal of Religion, Disability & Health* 12, (3) (2008): 236-250.

Catechism of the Catholic Church: Pocket Edition. London: Geoffrey Chapman, 1995.

Cole, Darrell. "Just War, Penance and the Church." *Pro Ecclesia* 11, no 3 (Sum 2002): 313-328.

Dorn, Christopher and John Zemmler. "The Invisible Wounds of War: Post-Traumatic Stress Disorder and Liturgy in Conversation." *Call to Worship* 43, no. 2 (2009-2010):1-8.

Douglas, Mary. *Purity and Danger: An Analysis of the Concepts of Purity and Taboo.* New York: Routledge, 1994.

Figley, Charles R. and William P. Nash, eds. *Combat Stress Injury: Theory, Research, and Management.* New York: Routledge, 2007.

Green, Robin. *Only Connect: Worship and Liturgy from the Perspective of Pastoral Care.* London: Darton, Longman and Todd, 1993.

Iasiello, Louis V. *Jus in Bellum: Key Issues for a Contemporary Assessment of Just Behavior in War,* PhD diss., Salve Regina University, 2003.

Litz, Brett T., Nathan Stein, Eileen Delaney, Leslie Lebowitz, William P. Nash, Caroline Silva and Shira Maguen, "Moral Injury and Moral Repair: A Preliminary Model and Intervention Strategy." *Clinical Psychology Review* 29 (2009): 695-706.

Luther, Martin. "Whether Soldiers, Too, Can Be Saved" in *Luther's Works: The Christian In Society,* vol. 46, Edited by Robert C. Schultz. Philadelphia: Fortress Press, 1967

McNeill, John T. and Helena M. Gamer. *Medieval Handbooks of Penance.* New York: Columbia University Press, 1938.

Merriam-Webster's Collegiate Dictionary, 11th Edition. Springfield, MA: Merriam- Webster, Inc. 2004

Nash, William P. "Combat/Operational Stress Adaptations and Injuries." In *Combat Stress Injury: Theory, Research, and Management,* edited by Charles R. Figley and William P. Nash, 33-63. New York: Routledge, 2007.

------. "The Stressors of War." in *Combat Stress Injury: Theory, Research, and Management,* edited by Charles R. Figley and William P. Nash, 11-31. New York: Routledge, 2007.

Nash, William and Dewleen G. Baker. "Competing and Complementary Models of Combat Stress Injury." in *Combat Stress Injury: Theory Research, and Management,* edited by Charles R. Figley and William P. Nash, 65-94. New York: Routledge, 2007.

Jacob Neusner, trans., *The Mishnah: The New Translation*. New Haven, CT: Yale University Press, 1988.

Proctor, John. "Proselytes and Pressure Cookers: The Meaning and Application of Acts 15:20." *International Review of Mission* (Oct. 1, 1996): 469-483.

Selby, Gary S. "The Meaning and Function of συνείδησις in Hebrews 9 and 10" in *Restoration Quarterly* 28, no. 3 (1985-1986): 145-154.

Shay, Jonathan. *Achilles in Vietnam: Combat Trauma and the Undoing of Character*. New York: Scribner, 1994.

------. "Casualties." *Daedalus* 140.3 (2011): 179-188.

------. *Odysseus in America: Combat Trauma and the Trials of Homecoming*. New York: Scribner, 2002.

Sippola, John, Amy Blumenshine, Donald Tubesing, and Valerie Yancy. *Welcome Them Home Help Them Heal: Pastoral Care and Ministry with Service Members Returning from War*. Duluth, Minnesota: Whole Person Associates, 2009.

Strong, James. *Strong's Exhaustive Concordance of the Bible*. 1890

Struthers, William M. *Wired for Intimacy*. Downers Grove, IL: Intervarsity Press, 2009.

Tanielian, Terri and Lisa H. Jaycox, eds. *The Invisible Wounds of War: Psychological and Cognitive Injuries, Their Consequences, and Services to Assist Recovery*. Santa Monica, CA: Rand Corporation, 2008.

Tick, Edward. *War and the Soul: Healing Our Nation's Veterans from Post-Traumatic Stress Disorder*. Wheaton, Illinois: Quest Books, 2005.

Verkamp, Bernard J. *The Moral Treatment of Returning Warriors in Early Medieval and Modern Times*. Scranton, Pennsylvania: University of Scranton Press, 2006.

------. "Moral Treatment of Returning Warriors in the Early Middle Ages," *Journal of Religious Ethics* 16, no. 2 (Fall 1988): 223-249.

Wright, David P. "Purification from Corpse-Contamination in Numbers XXXI, 19-24," *Vetus Testamentum* 35, 2 (1985): 213-223.

Zanchettin, Leo, ed. "A Sign that Heals." *The Word Among Us* 31, no. 6 (June 2012): 4-9.

ELECTRONIC SOURCES

Al Arabiya News, "Bush denies he is an 'enemy of Islam'", (Oct 5, 2007) http://www.alarabiya.net/articles/2007/10/05/39989.html (accessed Sept 30, 2013)

Bender, Laura, "An Order for Welcoming Service Members Returning from War." (May 2007). http://www.gbhem.org/site/apps/nlnet/content2.aspx?c=lsKSL3PO LvF&b=5079785&ct=4969667 (Accessed May 18, 2011).

------. "An Order for Blessing Service Members Deploying to War." http://www.gbhem.org/site/apps/nlnet/content2.aspx?c=lsKSL3PO LvF&b=5079785&ct=4969669 (accessed June 3, 2012).

Dao, James "Back From War, Fear and Danger Fill Driver's Seat", New York Times, (Jan 10, 2012) http://www.nytimes.com/2012/01/11/us/post-traumatic-stress-disorder-may-cause-erratic-driving.html?pagewanted=all&_r=0 (accessed May 16, 2014)

Falzone, Diana "Should Military Marriages Include a 'Deployment Sex Pact'?" FoxNews.Com (Nov 12, 2012) http://www.foxnews.com/opinion/2012/11/26/military-marriages-and-deployment-sex-pact/ (accessed Oct 5,2013)

General Board of Church and Society of the United Methodist Church "Paragraph 165 VI C: The World Community" *Social Principles* http://umc-gbcs.org/social-principles/165-vi.-the-world-community (accessed May 22, 2014)

Gilbert, Kathy L. "Chaplains: Church must support returning soldiers" *United Methodist News Service* (Feb. 20, 2007) http://www.umc.org/site/apps/nl/content3.asp?c=lwL4KnN1LtH&b=2429867&ct=3574065 (accessed Dec. 13, 2012).

Johansmeyer,Tom. "Operation Desert Porn" in Boston Magazine
(July 2008)
http://www.bostonmagazine.com/articles/operation_desert_porn/pa
ge2 (accessed Aug 23, 2011).

Kaiser, Dakota J. "Combat Related Post Traumatic Stress Disorder in
Veterans of Operation Enduring Freedom and Operation Iraqi
Freedom: A Review of the Literature" (June 24, 2012) *Graduate Journal
of Counseling Psychology*, Vol 3, no. 1,
http://epublications.marquette.edu/gjcp/vol3/iss1/5 (accessed on
Dec 18, 2012)

North American Missions Board of the Southern Baptist Convention. "A
Biblical Response To Post Traumatic Stress Disorder (PTSI)." (2009).
http://www.namb.net/chaplaincyresources (accessed April 5, 2011).

Operation Barnabas. From the link "Service Of Welcome For A Returning
Veteran." http://barnabas.lcmsworldmission.org/?page_id=624,
(accessed Dec. 13, 2012).

Slack, Charles. "PTSD Timeline: Centuries of Trauma," *Protomag* (Summer
2010). http://protomag.com/assets/ptsd-timeline-centuries-of-traum
(accessed Nov. 18, 2010).

9
APPENDIX

Lincoln's Second Inaugural Address
Saturday, March 4, 1865

Fellow Countrymen:

At this second appearing to take the oath of the presidential office, there is less occasion for an extended address than there was at the first. Then a statement, somewhat in detail, of a course to be pursued, seemed fitting and proper. Now, at the expiration of four years, during which public declarations have been constantly called forth on every point and phase of the great contest which still absorbs the attention, and engrosses the energies of the nation, little that is new could be presented. The progress of our arms, upon which all else chiefly depends, is as well known to the public as to myself; and it is, I trust, reasonably satisfactory and encouraging to all. With high hope for the future, no prediction in regard to it is ventured.

On the occasion corresponding to this four years ago, all thoughts were anxiously directed to an impending civil-war. All dreaded it -- all sought to avert it. While the inaugural address was being delivered from this place, devoted altogether to saving the Union without war, insurgent agents were in the city seeking to destroy it without war -- seeking to dissolve the Union, and divide effects, by negotiation. Both parties deprecated war; but one of them would make war rather than let the nation survive; and the other would accept war rather than let it perish. And the war came.

One eighth of the whole population were colored slaves, not distributed generally over the Union, but localized in the Southern part of it. These slaves constituted a peculiar and powerful interest. All knew that this interest was, somehow, the cause of the war. To strengthen, perpetuate, and extend this interest was the object for which the insurgents would rend the

Union, even by war; while the Government claimed no right to do more than to restrict the territorial enlargement of it. Neither party expected for the war, the magnitude, or the duration, which it has already attained. Neither anticipated that the cause of the conflict might cease with, or even before, the conflict itself should cease. Each looked for an easier triumph, and a result less fundamental and astounding. Both read the same Bible, and pray to the same God; and each invokes His aid against the other. It may seem strange that any men should dare to ask a just God's assistance in wringing their bread from the sweat of other men's faces; but let us judge not that we be not judged. The prayers of both could not be answered; that of neither has been answered fully. The Almighty has His own purposes. "Woe unto the world because of offenses! for it must needs be that offenses come; but woe to that man by whom the offense cometh!" If we shall suppose that American Slavery is one of those offenses which, in the providence of God, must needs come, but which, having continued through His appointed time, He now wills to remove, and that He gives to both North and South, this terrible war, as the woe due to those by whom the offense came, shall we discern therein any departure from those divine attributes which the believers in a Living God always ascribe to Him? Fondly do we hope -- fervently do we pray -- that this mighty scourge of war may speedily pass away. Yet, if God wills that it continue, until all the wealth piled by the bond-man's two hundred and fifty years of unrequited toil shall be sunk, and until every drop of blood drawn with the lash, shall be paid by another drawn with the sword, as was said three thousand years ago, so still it must be said "the judgments of the Lord, are true and righteous altogether."

With malice toward none; with charity for all; with firmness in the right, as God gives us to see the right, let us strive on to finish the work we are in; to bind up the nation's wounds; to care for him who shall have borne the battle, and for his widow, and his orphan -- to do all which may achieve and cherish a just, and a lasting peace, among ourselves, and with all nations.

ABOUT THE AUTHOR

David Bachelor is the Director of Warrior Wash Ministry, a non-profit organization that conducts retreats for veterans wounded by posttraumatic stress. He is a veteran of Iraq and Afghanistan and still serves in the Navy Reserves. He and his wife Glenda live in New Mexico and have three grown children.

He can be contacted at www.thewarriorwash.com

Made in the USA
Charleston, SC
05 July 2016